Called and Chosen for Destiny

WORKBOOK

Authored By
Joan E. Murray

Joan Murray Ministries

Called and Chosen for Destiny

Workbook

Knowing and Fulfilling Your Destiny in God

But ye are a chosen generation, a royal priesthood, a holy nation, a peculiar people; that ye should show forth the praises of Him who hath called you out of darkness into His marvelous light.

1 Peter 2:9 (KJV)

Called and Chosen for Destiny

ISBN 978-1-963016-25-3

EBOOK ISBN 978-1-963016-26-0

For permission contact Joan Murray Ministries @
jmmcontactus@gmail.com

Published in the United States of America

Table of Contents

Introduction

As I think back over my life, I have wondered many times why my existence seemed so ordinary. I have had a clear understanding that God handcrafted me for a great destiny but have often felt that my existence was merely mediocre. Like me, I know that many of you have a great desire to step out of the ordinary and into something extraordinary, fulfilling, and beneficial. You desire to step into greatness but are unsure of the steps that will lead you down the path to ultimate fulfillment. As I contemplated my ordinary existence, I came to realize that ordinary was not for me, and it should not be for you either. It was liberating to discover that if I were the only person on earth, God would still have sent Jesus, and He would have died that painful and horrible death just for me. The same holds true for you as well.

I came to understand that a loving Father had adopted me into His family. This adoption came because His Son was willing to be born into an earthly family where He became the adopted Son of a carpenter. By His death, He provided a way for us to be adopted by God. It was also great news when I discovered that in previous centuries, although a natural born son could be disinherited, a son or daughter by adoption could never be disinherited. God Himself has adopted and given you His name, an inheritance and a destiny, and He will never abandon nor disinherit you. He has provided for you an opportunity to walk away from a mediocre and ordinary existence into a great calling and an even greater destiny. God has called, chosen, and destined you to live life brimming with an abundance of joy, peace, health, and wealth. As you discover this life, which is filled with destiny, you will discover something beyond the ordinary.

Many times, on the way to your destiny, you may encounter some disappointments, discouragement, and even despair, which have been sent by the enemy to derail and keep you living below your privileges as heirs to a great inheritance. However, as sons and daughters of God, you must know who you are and understand your rightful place. You are children of the King and are designed for greatness in Him. Therefore, you must be tenacious and determine in your heart that you will not be stopped, deterred, or derailed. You will be victorious in all areas of life and will fulfill the great calling and destiny that God has placed on your life.

The book you hold in your hand contains signposts to help you achieve your greatest destiny in God. It is my passion to help people realize how truly valuable they are and the high price God paid to get them back into right relationship with Him. If you truly desire to experience fullness in your life and to walk completely in God's amazing blessings and provisions for your destiny, you must fully accept how greatly loved you are. As you read, believe and apply the principles and insights from this book, expect God to take you into a deeper, more intimate relationship with Him. In this new intimacy, you will discover a new and deeper level of your purpose, your passion, and your life's calling. You will discover that God desires your total fulfillment in every area of your life. I therefore invite you to dig deeply into the pages of this book to discover the roadmap that will lead you on an adventure to your destination, which will be worth your pursuit and your total commitment.

Joan Murray

Chapter 1: Called by God

.... that you may declare the praises of Him who called you out of darkness into His wonderful light.

1 Peter 2:9b (NIV)

God has called you to fulfill a great destiny. It is a destiny that He deposited in your heart before He placed you in your mother's womb. When you first realized something significant was missing in your life and you asked Jesus to come into your heart, this destiny was fully manifested in you. The moment He entered, He began by replacing all the negative thoughts and ideas that were planted in you by the devil.

Thoughts of:

- *Doubt was replaced with confidence and assurance.*
- *Fear was replaced with faith.*
- *Unbelief was replaced by a trust in a God who has abundant supplies.*
- *Worry was replaced with the knowledge that He will never leave you or forsake you.*

God's re-entrance into your life causes you to be dissatisfied with an ordinary existence. You have come to the realization that He has not called you to live a mediocre existence, but a life filled with confidence and faith. Because God has called you, there is a sense of dissatisfaction when you settle for less than what is in your heart to do. God tugs at your heart so you will not settle for less than the blessings, provisions, and destiny He mapped out for your life. A loving Father, who does not want you to settle for an unremarkable existence, placed the longing you experience to do more, in your heart. *1 Peter 2:9b - ....That you may declare the praises of Him who called you out of darkness into His marvelous light.*

This scripture explains why God called you. You were living in darkness, away from His light; and He invited you to come closer so you could experience how living in His light could bring you hope, joy, refreshing, peace, and fullness. His light illuminates your path and leads you down the best pathway for your life. He has called you to experience Him in all His fullness and His glory. When you answered His call, you said, "yes" to His plans, "yes" to His ways, and "yes" to His will for your life. Repeat this to yourself, *"I am called, sanctified, and set apart for God's use. I am singled out, and I am of the finest quality because I am created in the image of the Father, Son and Holy Spirit."*

What dreams has God called you to fulfill?

____

____

____

____

____

____

How can you discover your dreams?

____

____

____

____

____

____

To be Called

.....that you may declare the praises of Him who called you out of darkness into His wonderful light.

1 Peter 2:9b (NIV)

All of you have been called by God to accomplish great things with your lives. He has called you to be a part of something greater than what you could ever imagine or think. You have been programmed by God with the desire to reach for more than just the things you have already attained. It seems, however, that this "something" keeps eluding you. I have discovered in my journey that the desire you have for more is the desire to know God at a deeper level and in a more intimate way. As you get to know Him, you will begin to discover the greater things that you feel a longing to attain. Before you were born, He called and made an appointment with you for the fulfillment of your destiny (Jeremiah 1:5). You have been called, sanctified, and set apart for use by God. He called and selected you above all others to do something for Him. You are His preferred and chosen child whom He singled out for a specific assignment that only you can fulfill. In singling you out, He wants you to understand that you are made of the finest quality materials. You are made in the likeness of the Father, Son, and Holy Spirit.

How do you accept the call to dream?

____

____

____

____

____

____

Many are Called

For many are called...

Matthew 22:14a (KJV)

The Bible specifically states that many are called. Before God called and selected you, you were lost, alone, and far away from Him. Then His voice resounded throughout the earth calling you into a relationship with Him.

In this relationship, you have complete access into His Presence and can share your heart, your desires, and your concerns with Him. As you open yourself to Him, He will share the reason for His call and the great plans He has for your life. Understand that God calls out to all humanity. He does not limit His call to just a few. Everyone that God created received this call to share the riches of His Kingdom. He called you for a specific destiny that He has programmed you to fulfill. His call is an invitation for you to come and hear more about your destiny.

Consider Adam and Eve the first people who received this call from God. When they heard His call, they must have responded quickly and with great excitement. I imagine that they had great expectations about having an audience with the Creator. They would have an opportunity to meet with Him face-to-face so that He could speak His destiny for them directly into their hearts. In their meetings with Him they would have learned how to rule and govern the planet. Since God is all knowing, He knew that they would not fully embrace the call that He had placed on their lives. He also knew that though they responded to His call initially, they would subsequently answer another call, which would ultimately lead them away from His plans and provisions for them and mankind.

Why do you think God has called many people?

____

____

____

____

____

____

Accepting the Call

The Lord had said to Abram, "Leave you country, your people and your father's household and go to the land I will show you. I will make you into a great nation and I will bless you, I will make your name great, and you will be a blessing. I will bless those who bless you, and whoever curses you I will curse, and all peoples on the earth will be blessed through you. So Abram left, as the Lord had told him; and Lot went with him. Abram was seventy-five years old when he set out from Haran.

Genesis 12: 1-4 (KJV)

All of us must listen and then respond to God's call. We have to make a decision to answer when He calls. When He called Abram, He gave him some specific instructions in order that he might walk fully into His calling/destiny.

God told him:

- Leave your country – leave your familiar surroundings
- Leave your people – separate from your family
- Leave your father's household – leave your place of provision and your comfort zone

After Abram accepted these instructions and was willing to make the sacrifice for his calling, God then gave him some promises:

- He would make him a great nation
- He would bless him
- He would make his name great
- He would bless the people who blessed him

- He would curse those who cursed him
- All people of the earth will be blessed because of Abram

Abram accepted the call, but he did not totally follow all the instructions. He took his nephew Lot with him even though God told him to separate from His family. As a result, he experienced some challenges with Lot. When you hear and accept God's call for your life, be willing to follow Him completely with the understanding that He knows what is ahead of you, and that He has made the right provisions for your arrival. Remember that any deviation from His instructions can cause you some severe hardship. Ask him to help you to clearly follow where He leads, and however He leads. When you trust Him, He will lead you safely to your destination.

Where should you begin your search for your dream?

____

____

____

____

____

____

What dreams/destinies are hidden in you?

____

____

____

____

____

Personal Notes/Reflection

Life Application:

1. Embrace the fact that God has called you to fulfill great things for Him.
2. Know that many are called. Accept your calling.

Chapter 2: Why Has God Called You?

Before I formed you in the womb I knew you, before you were born I set you apart, I appointed you as a prophet to the nations.

Jeremiah 1:5 (KJV)

Many of us have wondered why God has called us.

- What does God want from us?
- Does He think I am qualified for His call?

God wants us to fulfill the destiny He so carefully planted in our hearts before He birthed us. The scriptures tell us clearly that He knew you prior to the selecting the womb, the parents, the city, the country, and the nationality of your birth. It is evident that you existed in God and He made a specific assignment for your life. Not only did he choose where you will begin life and with whom, He qualified you for the call He placed in your heart. He called you, He chose you and He has anointed, and appointed you to fulfill every destiny He birthed you to fulfill. He called you to fulfill a specific purpose in Him, it is a purpose only you can fulfill. No one else has been qualified, appointed or anointed by God to fulfill this purpose but you. He is waiting for you to begin the journey. Every step you take, He will be right there with you cheering you all the way to the finish line. Begin the walk and listen for the cheers.

Can anyone else truly fulfill my destiny as well as I can?

____

____

____

____

____

His Dream – Your Dream

And it shall come to pass afterward, that I will pour out my spirit upon all flesh; and you sons and your daughters shall prophesy, your old men shall dream dreams, your young men shall see visions.

Joel 2:28 (KJV)

- Do you know that God has a dream for your life?
- Have you discovered His personal dream for you life?

God does have an amazing dream and plan for your life. His vision for you was placed in your heart prior to selecting your earthly parents. He has a dream and a plan for *every life.* He did not forget a single person when He was giving out dream assignments. There is a desire in your heart to do more and to have more out of life. To find out what this desire is, I invite you to go on a treasure hunt.

- As a child, what were your interest, talent and passion?
- What did you love doing?
- What things came naturally to you while growing up?
- What have you always been passionate about and still are today?

These interests, talents, and passions are a clue to the dream assignment God has for your life. Your dream is yours alone, and no one can fulfill it for you. God chose you personally for this dream, and He is counting on you for its fulfillment. No one else can fulfill your dream assignment in the way that God intended it to be fulfilled by you.

I encourage you to make a decision to complete every dream assignment God puts in your heart. Do not die with your dreams unfulfilled. Dr. Myles Munroe says it best – he said, "The richest place on earth is the graveyard." Why is this so?" Because many have died with their dreams and the destinies God planned for their lives, unfulfilled. Declare to yourself that this will never be you. You will indeed fulfill all the assignments God assigned for your life.

What dream has God called me to fulfill?

____

____

____

____

____

Called to Dream

Joseph, a young man of seventeen, was tending the flocks with his brothers, the sons of Bilhah and the sons of Zilpah, his father's wives, and he brought their father a bad report about them. Now Israel (Jacob) loved Joseph more than any of his other sons, because he had been born to him in his old age; and he made a richly ornamented robe for him.

Genesis 37:2-4 (NIV)

When his brothers saw that their father loved him more than any of them, they hated him and could not speak a kind word to him.

I love the story of Joseph the dreamer. Here was a young man who knew how to dream and believed in dreams. His very name meant, "May God add," so it is evident that he was always looking to God to add more to his life. Joseph was a favored son, and this favoritism caused jealousy among his brothers. His brothers hated him because he found favor with his father. Then it appeared he found favor with God because God began to speak to him about dreams and destiny. He was only seventeen years old and did not yet understand that he should not share his dreams and visions with just anyone. What Joseph and so many of us have discovered is that often people will not rejoice with us about the things God is speaking and revealing to our hearts about our destiny. In his dream Joseph saw his brothers bowing down before him, and then he saw eleven stars and the sun and moon bowing down before him. The eleven stars represented the other eleven tribes of Israel, while the sun and moon represented his father and mother. His brothers wanted to kill him but were unable to do so. When God places dreams and visions in your heart, the enemy cannot destroy you because those dreams and visions must be fulfilled. That statement should boost your confidence to know that whatever difficulty you face, if you stay connected to God, your destiny will keep you and your dream alive until its fulfillment.

How do I know that God has personally called me?

____

____

____

The Preferred Choice

But God demonstrates his own love for us in this: While we were still sinners, Christ died for us.

Romans 5:8 (NIV)

Do you know that you are God's preferred choice? Go ahead and say it. "I am God's preferred choice." The passage above is clear about the love God has for you. While you were still in sin, God sent Christ to die for you. Consider the fact that this preferential treatment is how God has chosen to demonstrate His great love and forgiveness toward you. Through the death of His Son, He forever revealed that you are His preferred choice. He demonstrated His preference by adopting you into His family. God took a fancy to you and chose to make you His own.

Why does God prefer you?

____

____

____

Called to Worship

Yet a time is coming and has now come when the true worshipers will worship the Father in spirit and truth, for they are the kind of worshipers that the Father seeks.

John 4:23 (NIV)

You were created, called, and designed to worship God. He called you to demonstrate His praises throughout the whole world. The Father seeks after true believers, those with hearts set on Him, who are neither ashamed nor afraid to give Him their highest worship. Worship is your calling; therefore, you must have a heart to get into the Presence of God regularly, to adore, reverence, and lift Him up. Worship is deep intimacy with God. It is allowing God to look into your heart as you pour your life out to Him. And it is also seeing the love, the forgiveness, and the mercy that fills His heart for you. In worship, you kneel in the presence of the one and only King, as you pay Him homage. You demonstrate your humility and your awe of His greatness and His amazing goodness. As you worship God, it takes your focus off your concerns and yourself and places it on the One who can provide a way of escape from your difficulties.

How do I answer God's call to worship?

Personal Notes/Reflection

Life Application:

1. Understand that you were designed to worship God.
2. God has sanctified you for use in His Kingdom.

Chapter 3: Chosen By God

Chosen By Adoption

He predestined us to be adopted, as His sons/daughters through Jesus Christ, in accordance with His pleasure and will to the praise of His glorious grace which He has fully given us in the One He loves.

Ephesians 1:5 (KJV)

You and I have been adopted into the family of God. Our adoption came because Jesus was willing to be born and then adopted into Joseph's earthly family for our redemption. Before time began, God predestined us to be adopted as His sons and daughters. He did it because it brought Him pleasure to have us in His family once again.

The sins of our forefather, Adam, caused separation between God and man; but the death of Jesus brought us back into right relationship and fellowship with Him. Adoption speaks of a love so deep that a person would willingly choose to take on total responsibility of another person's life and welfare. God chose to allow Jesus to suffer in our place so that through His suffering we could be in close fellowship and relationship with Him once again.

God so loved us that no price was too steep for Him to pay in exchange for us. Adoption in previous centuries was an amazing gift to the adoptee, and it still is today. In previous centuries, an adopted child could NEVER be disinherited! You can never be disinherited!!! You belong to God always and forever. No one, no circumstance, no situation, and no hardship will be able to separate you from God. That should bring great peace and assurance to your heart.

Do I truly understand that I belong to God?

____

____

____

____

____

____

Chosen by Love

For God so loved the world that He gave His only begotten Son that whosoever believeth in Him should not perish but have everlasting life.

John 3:16 (KJV)

Love!!! The word brings to mind many emotions. Many of us have experienced its joys, sorrows, and pains; but the love we will focus on today is the love that fills us with joy, hope, peace and rest.
God so loved.... God's love is agape love. Agape loves is:

- Steadfast
- Unfailing
- Unchanging
- A love that is constant

God's love for man is steadfast, unfailing, unchanging and constant. Because His love is so great toward man, He allowed Jesus to suffer a horrible death so we could experience His amazing, undeserved love in our lives. Because of His great love, it is clear that, when we love, the fruit of love is giving. Love causes us to give of our time, efforts, resources, and ourselves. The love the Father has for His children is a love that is timeless -- a love that keeps on giving even when we mess up and miss the mark. His love never stops giving to us. It is in constant pursuit of us.

God so loved (you – add your name) that He gave His one and only Son just for you; and, if you were the only person on planet earth, He would have still given His one and only Son's life for yours. What great love the Father has for you!!

How deep and how wide is God's love for you (add your name)?

____

____

____

____

____

____

Chosen To Follow God

So, Abram left, as the Lord had told him; and Lot went with him. Abram was seventy-five years old when he set out from Haran. He took his wife Sarai, his nephew Lot, all the possessions they had accumulated and the people they had acquired in Haran, and they set out for the land of Canaan, and they arrived there.

Genesis 12:4-5 (KJV)

God chose Abraham to follow Him into a fulfilling destiny. God uprooted Abraham from his familiar surroundings and removed him from his family and friends to train him for his destiny. Abraham's destiny required total dependence on God for its fulfillment. Although this move was difficult, Abraham believed he heard the voice of God and moved out in faith.

Believe, when you hear the voice of God, and move out in faith. Hearing God's voice is the key to your step of faith. No one can accurately tell you what God is saying about your destiny – only the all-knowing God can reveal this. Others may confirm that God is speaking to you, but you must hear Him for yourself and act on His leading. God has chosen you to follow Him, and His path for your life. When you understand that your steps are ordered of God, you will have the courage to step out in faith to fulfill all that He has in store for you.

God orders your steps – you have to make a step toward your destiny so God can align you on the path that will lead you to a life of fullness and a life overflowing with His abundant blessings. Choose to follow God closely and watch how He will amaze you and others with His perfect plan for your life.

How do I leave all and totally follow God?

____

____

____

____

____

____

Chosen By A Dream

Joseph had a dream, and when he told it to his brothers, they hated him all the more. He said to them, "Listen to this dream I had: We were binding sheaves of grain out in the field when suddenly my sheaf rose and stood upright, while your sheaves gathered around mine and bowed down to it." His brothers said to him, "Do you intend to reign over us? Will you actually rule us?" And they hated him all the more because of his dream and what he had said. Then he had another dream, and he told it to his brothers. "Listen," he said, "I had another dream, and this time the sun and moon and eleven stars were bowing down to me."

Genesis 37: 5-9 (NIV)

God still speaks to us in dreams, as He did with Joseph centuries ago. God gave Joseph a vision of his life's purpose and destiny in a dream. Although

Joseph did not fully understand the dream, he knew God was speaking to him; and he embraced what he heard.

In his excitement, Joseph shared his dream with his brothers; and it caused him much trouble and heartache. They tried to kill him but sold him into slavery instead. While in Egypt, Joseph was a slave in his master's house; and God used these difficult times of his life to develop character in him. This process caused him to lead with integrity. God used the suffering he experienced to develop compassion not only for his brothers but also for the people he was assigned to serve.

God uses dreams. He plants dreams in the hearts of His children; and He invites us to embrace them, to believe them, and to guard them. Like Joseph, God will allow us to experience difficulties that He uses to prepare and equip us to fulfill His dreams for our lives. I encourage you to prepare your hearts to hear, receive, and obey when God clearly speaks to you.

What did God have in mind when He chose me?

____

____

____

____

____

Personal Notes/Reflection

Life Application:

1. Welcome and embrace the fact that God has chosen you for a great purpose in Him.
2. You are adopted by God to be a part of His family.

Chapter 4: Rest For The Chosen

So, I declared on oath in my anger, "They shall never enter my rest."

Hebrews 3:11(NIV)

It appears as if God was denying rest to His people in this scripture, but that is not the case. God was trying to give the Israelites, His chosen people, rest from all their laboring and striving but they simply would not receive it. They were accomplishing nothing of value for God and themselves because they depended on their own strength and power. Coming out of Egyptian bondage, being slaves for years, they could not conceive that it was possible to enjoy life without the daily struggles they had endured.

God desired to give them "true rest." This rest is one He had so lovingly provided for them so they would not have to work and toil. He provided their daily food, their clothes did not wear out, and He protected them day and night; but they could not fully receive all His provisions.
In anger, God declared that they would never enter His rest. It was the Father's frustration because they were not able to receive the provisions that were available to them. Although God was angry, He still loved the Israelites and had tremendous compassion for them.

God wants to give you the same degree of rest. He knows the hardships you have faced and are facing; and He invites you, just as He did the Israelites, to come and enter into His rest. This rest is a place where you can trust Him with your health, your finances, your family, and all the secret longings of your soul. He is extremely faithful and because you are His, He wants you to trust Him to bring about His best results in your life. Are you willing to rest in Him today?

How can I completely embrace the rest of God in my life?

____

____

____

____

____

____

A Rest Of Faith

"Come to me, all you who are weary and burdened, and I will give you rest. Take my yoke upon you and learn from me, for I am gentle and humble in heart, and you will find rest for you souls. For my yoke is easy and my burden is light."

Matthew 11:28 – 30 (NIV)

Rest!!! Do you long to experience total rest for you mind, emotions and heart? God desires to give you the same rest that He so lovingly provided to the Israelites. He has seen your struggles and how burdened you have become with the trials of life. He bids you to come to Him to find strength when you are weary, hope when you feel burdened, and rest so that you can live in health and prosper in all areas of your life.

God wants to take the heavy yoke that you are carrying, which is too burdensome, and replace it with His rest. A burden is like a backpack that children take to school. It is manageable and easy for them to transport. Many of our burdens are bearable, but we can go to God and cast them on Him and let Him handle them.

A yoke, however, is far weightier. In previous centuries they would yoke an old and younger donkey together so they could pull the yoke together. The older donkey was training the younger one how to manage his yoke. God wants to yoke-up with you so that you will no longer be burdened with a heavy load. He desires to give you peace where you are experiencing none, to give you hope where you feel hopeless, and to provide you with help so that in your daily life you can experience His amazing rest of faith. In the midst of every struggle, difficulty or trial, rest in Him. He will draw you close to Him and handle your cares Himself.

What is keeping me from experiencing God's true rest?

____

____

____

____

____

____

Times of Testing

Don't love money; be satisfied with what you have. For God has said, "I will never fail you. I will never abandon you."

Hebrews 13:5 (NLT)

Many of us have wondered during seasons of testing if God is really with us. This scripture promises that God will never leave us or forsake us. He is an ever-present help in times of trouble. Jesus told us that in this life we will have tribulation (trials, troubles, and difficulties), but to be of good cheer because He has overcome the world. Trouble comes to all of us not always because of something we have done wrong, but because sin is in the world and sin affects us all. But Jesus! He gives us a promise that even when we are troubled we can be cheerful and have joy and peace. This is possible because He is with us in the middle of our troubles.

When the three Hebrew boys (Shadrack, Meshach, and Abednego) were thrown into the deadly fiery furnace, the Lord was waiting for them. They did not go through their difficulty alone.

Life may seem as if you are on a never-ending cycle of trouble and difficulty; but even in the midst of them, God is right there with you. He will never leave you to face trials by yourself. The word 'never' means 'at no time' will He ever leave you. Everyone may walk away from you, when you face trouble; but God is a constant help, a constant support and a constant presence in your life. He is your place of safety no matter what you are facing. Rest in His promises because He is available for you always!

How can you find rest in the midst of trouble?

Personal Notes/Reflection

Life Application:

1. God wants you to find true rest in Him.
2. God plans for you to enjoy the provisions that can be found by faith in Him.

Chapter 5: Who Are You?

Then God said, "Let us make man in our image, in our likeness, and let them rule over the fish of the sea and the birds of the air, over the livestock, over all the earth, and over all the creatures that move along the ground." So God created man in His own image, in the image of God He created him; male and female He created them. God blessed them and said to them, "Be fruitful and increase in number; fill the earth and subdue it. Rule over the fish of the sea and the birds of the air and over every living creature that moves on the ground."

Genesis 1:26 – 28 (KJV)

You are created in the image of God the Father, God the Son, and God the Holy Spirit. Each has a separate, distinct personality and role. God created all that we see around the earth. Jesus, our Savior, gave His all for us. The Holy Spirit is our Helper, our Comforter, the ONE who guides our lives, and is the enforcer of God's will on earth.

God gave you the ability to speak things into existence in your life. Jesus gave His life to redeem you; therefore, you are also a 'giver' by nature. The power of the Holy Spirit gives you wisdom and guidance to live a successful life. You belong exclusively to God as you have been created and marked (sealed) in His image.

Because God loves you, He will not withhold any good thing from you. He has made a significant deposit of Himself in every believer's heart and life. When you accepted Jesus into your hearts, the Holy Spirit came to dwell in you so you would have the power and ability to become all God has created you to be. Remember, you are a masterpiece and were created to represent God to all people on earth so you must remember to act like your Creator.

Who does God say you are?

____

____

____

____

____

____

The Image of Jesus

In the beginning was the Word, and the Word was with God, and the Word was God, He was with God in the beginning.

John 1:1-2 (KJV)

Jesus was in the very beginning with the Father. When God said let us make man in our image, He was referring to Jesus, the Holy Spirit and Himself. I call this the ultimate board meeting.

God sent Jesus to give His life for you. As a result, you are free from the grip of sin. Jesus is the giver of life but also of many blessings and gifts that the Father has reserved for His children. He freely gave of Himself to teach us how to give of ourselves to others. To be in the image of Jesus means you reflect Him beautifully to the world. When the people of the world see you, they should see a person filled with:

- Joy
- Peace
- Hope
- Love
- Compassion
- Forgiveness

All of these attributes are a reflection of the character of Jesus. He exemplified all of these characteristics; and He demonstrates to you a clear example of how you also can live out these attributes in your life.

The scripture says that the 'Word' – Jesus -- was in the beginning with God. It further states that the Word was God. It is clear that Jesus and the Father are one even though they have different administration and functions. They act as one, they work in unity with each other, and they take care of the needs of those who belong to them with the help of the Holy Spirit. While He was on earth, Jesus did not act on His own - He only did what the Father instructed Him to do. We must also do only what the Father instructs us to do. When we obey Him, we show Him that we are exactly like His Son; and we desire to please Him.

How can I be a true reflection of Jesus?

____

____

____

____

A Worshipper

Come let us worship and bow down, let us kneel before the Lord our maker.

Psalm 95:6 (KJV)

To be a worshiper is the key to how much you will experience God, discover who you are and fulfill the great destiny He has for you. You and I worship God primarily because He is absolutely deserving of our worship. He redeemed us by grace after Adam and Eve sinned and gave up their authority to the enemy. God did not let us live out eternity in pain, grief, and suffering.

We should have suffered for our sins but we were released from its penalty because of the victory of Jesus over death, hell, and the grave.

We worship God because Jesus' is continuously interceding for us. He is concerned about the situations that we are in, the things that are painful for us to bear, and for the conditions of our lives. He is always praying for us and seeking God's mercies on our behalf.

We worship God because:

- He loves us
- We love Him
- He is the One and only God
- We have surrendered our lives to Him

- We respect Him
- We adore Him
- We reverence Him
- We honor Him

There are many reasons we worship God; and you will find that in your personal relationship with Him there are many other reasons that will cause you to bow your knees in total admiration of who He is in your life and for all He will do for you. He is God and is completely worthy of our worship.

How can I surrender my all in worship to God?

____

____

____

____

____

____

An Heir Of God

So you are no longer a slave, but a son; and since you are a Son of God; God has made you also an heir.

Galatians 4:7 (KJV)

Now if we are children, then we are heirs – heirs of God and co-heirs with Christ.

Romans 8:17a (KJV)

We are heirs of God and joint-heirs with Jesus Christ. This means that whatever God has given to Jesus is also ours. We have joint ownership with Him. The good news is that we don not have to wait to inherit the promises of God for our lives. There are thousands of promises in the Word, and we can claim them all as an heir of God.

As joint-heirs with Jesus, we can claim our inheritances NOW. Since Jesus has already died, we do not have to wait for those inheritances. When we receive an inheritance from our earthly parents, the inheritance does not change hands until they die. As sons (and daughters) of God, we have access to all the blessings God has provided for us here on earth because of the death of His son.

Heirs ...

- are beneficiaries to a kingdom – Jesus prepared it for us
- have the same blessings as Jesus
- have a legacy in God
- are able to legally claim their inheritance

We have the counsel of the Godhead because we are heirs of God, and this divine support and guidance helps us, as we pursue our destiny.

Nothing is impossible for God's heirs because His provisions and blessings are available for all of His children to enjoy.

How can I embrace and believe that I own the things that Jesus owns?

____

____

____

____

____

____

Personal Notes/Reflection

Life Application:

1. God has made you in His image so you look like Him.
2. You are important in the Kingdom of God.

Chapter 6: You Are Special!

You Are Special!

And even the very hairs of your head are all numbered.

Matthew 10:30 (KJV)

Do you love to hear that you are special? You are indeed special to God! God loves you in an amazing and wonderful way; and, if you were the only person on earth, God would still have sent Jesus to die just for you – this is love in its richest form.

Scientists say there are millions of sperm cells that approach the female egg in order for a child to be born. Consider this -- out of those millions, you were the one who made it!! You were the one specifically hand-selected by God to be born. You are amazingly special to God!

The scripture says that God numbered the hairs on your head. How many of you know the number of strands of hair that are on your head? God knows each and every one of them. He takes delight in you.

God handcrafted you. You do not look like anyone else, talk like anyone else, or have the same personality or make up as any one else. Your handprint, footprint, voiceprint are unlike anyone else's -- they are uniquely yours. You are exceptional to God, and you are exclusively designed for Him. The God of heaven knows how truly special you are and He did not make a carbon copy or replica of you. Even twins have different personalities and traits.

To say you are special does not cover the amazing work of art that you are. Celebrate who you are and know that there is no one else like you on planet earth.

How does God see me?

How special am I to God?

The Discovery

And wisdom and knowledge shall be the stability of thy times, and strength of salvation: The fear of the Lord is his treasure.

Isaiah 33:6 (KJV)

How many of you have discovered that there are hidden treasures in you? God has placed His stamp of approval on you. His very nature is in you. To discover what God has in store for your life, you must go on an adventure. You must search for the reason God created you to be who you are. He was very specific in your 'design' – He did not miss a detail for your life.

On your adventure, you will probably discover many things that you have been saying to the Lord about yourself that are not true. Many of you have been repeating what you have heard others say about you, but what they have said is not a true reflection of how God sees you and of who you are.

Some of us have said critical things about ourselves, but this is not how God sees us. We think we are not tall enough, short enough, small enough, and intelligent enough, this list can go on and on – you get the picture. God is telling you that you are exactly how He designed you to be and you have everything you need in you to fulfill your destiny. When you tell Him the things you don't like about yourself, what you are saying to Him is that He made a mistake in your 'design'. Imagine telling the King of the universe that He made a mistake, when He designed you!

You are not a surprise to God, and you are definitely not a disappointment. He loves you just as you are, and He welcomes you into His presence at all times. Begin to see yourself differently and then rewrite your 'self' script. Allow God to develop all the gifts and talents He placed in you.

What negative things have I been saying about myself?

____

____

____

____

____

____

A Royal Priesthood

But you are a chosen generation, a royal priesthood, a holy nation....

1 Peter 2:9a (KJV)

The Bible says you are a royal priesthood. This means you are part of a royal family of priests. You are of the family of God. Because of 'whose' you are, you stand out in a crowd. He who lives in you is the King of Kings and the Lord of lords.

In the Old Testament a high priest was consecrated to God. In the New Testament a high priest is not only consecrated but is holy, blameless and divine in nature. Jesus is our great high priest and He is holy and pure. He is our ultimate high priest.
You and I represent Jesus -- our high priest. The New Testament clearly teaches the priesthood of all believers. 1 Peter 2:5 says, "You also, like living stones, are being built into a spiritual house to be a holy priesthood,

offering spiritual sacrifices acceptable to God through Jesus Christ." This means that we share in all of Christ's priestly activities. Each time we share the Word of God with someone, we are acting as a priest in the Kingdom of God. When we bring people into a relationship with Jesus Christ, we are acting as priests.

As our High Priest, Jesus understands all of our needs and He is concerned about us. He daily speaks to God about us. We are never alone in the struggles we are facing. He is always with us! When we find ourselves in the midst of difficulties, if we look closely, we will find that He is ahead of us in the problem and already has the solutions prepared for us.

Our great High Priest, Jesus, is always available to us. He is not distant but is as close as the breath we breathe. Hold on tightly to Him and never let Him go.

What makes you different from the world?

____

____

____

____

A Holy Nation

But you are a chosen generation, a royal priesthood, a holy nation....

I Peter 2:9a (KJV)

When God calls us a holy nation of people, He is talking about a group of people He has consecrated for Himself. You are blessed because God has given you His blessings.

The Bible encourages us to be holy as He is holy (1 Peter 1:16). This means we have the privilege of living a holy life with the help of God. To be holy is to know that you are separated and set aside to be of special use in the service of God.

The Bible teaches that light and darkness cannot co-exist together. God is light; and we were living in darkness, so the two could not meet until the blood of Jesus washed, cleansed, and purified us.

Throughout the Bible, the word holiness is used to define the character of God. The word holy means to be saintly, sacred, and pure; and it defines the loving nature of God. It means that God is separate from evil. God personifies holiness in all of His attributes, and He calls you to live a life of holiness.

When Jesus walked the earth, evil spirits recognized Him as being holy because He is the Son of God with God's nature.

It is possible for us to live a holy and pleasing life because God lives in us. When we are faced with the choice to either do good or bad, He is there with the answers. When we ask for His help, God will help us to overcome temptation and will always provide the way of escape for us.

What does living holy means to you?

____

____

A Peculiar People

Who gave Himself for us to redeem us from all wickedness and to purify for Himself a people that are His very own, eager to do what is good.

Titus 2:14 (KJV)

Many of us have been called strange and unusual at times. This is a compliment for those who understand that what people are saying is they are having a difficult time understanding us.

God has called us His 'peculiar' people. We are His 'peculiar treasures'. When the world looks at us, they see people who live life differently from them. They don't understand us. We look and operate differently than the world. The world lives on a reverse system from ours, which is why they think we are strange and unusual. We confound their logical way of thinking because we do not act like them, when we are tried in the fires of adversity. When we choose to rejoice in the midst of grief and difficulties, the world considers us unusual. What they don't understand is that there is One who sustains us through it all. His name is **Jesus!**

You should be encouraged and celebrate who you are and know that you are amazing to God. He loves us as we are because you are just like Him!

What makes me special to God and others?

You Are A Giver

For God so love the world that He gave His only begotten Son, that whosoever believeth in Him should not perish, but have everlasting life.

John 3:16 (KJV)

But God demonstrates His own love for us in this: While we were still sinners Christ died for us.

Romans 5:8 (KJV)

We were created in the image of the 'giver of life'. The One we serve demonstrated His love for us through His giving. He gave of Himself in the form of His Son. We were designed not only to look like Him but also to act like Him.

The scriptures tell us clearly that -- because of love -- God gave and keeps on giving to us. Love is His motivation for giving to our lives. While we were lost, alone, and without hope, God sent His very best to redeem our lives.

Because of the nature of the One who lives in us, it is unnatural for believers not to have a heart to give.

We can give of our time, our effort, our resources and ourselves. When we are giving, we are fulfilled. When we step out of self, and meet the needs of others, we begin to fulfill God's purposes for our lives.

There are people who live to give. They live in our homes, on the mission fields, in our churches and communities. We were designed to be one of those people.

Why is it important that I give?

____

____

____

____

____

____

Personal Notes/Reflection

Life Application:

1. Believe that you are special to God.
2. You were created to be a giver just like God.

Chapter 7: Called and Chosen for Service

Called To Serve

Serve wholeheartedly, as if you were serving the Lord, not men, because you know that the Lord will reward everyone for whatever he does, whether he is slave or free.

Ephesians 6:7-8 (KJV)

We often see successes in certain industries because of the service they provide to meet the needs of people. We are designed to serve others. To serve effectively, we must want to serve; and we must determine to serve with our whole heart.

When you begin to serve, you have to decide to pour yourself into every assignment. You give your best service when you realize that you are serving God and not man. Men receive the blessings of your service to the Lord, but God will reward you for every good deed you perform.

God has called us to serve others. We serve in our homes, on the job, in church, in school, in ministry, etc. It is the highest calling of our life to serve people -- whether they are small or great, bound or free.

Jesus is our perfect example of service. He came to earth for one purpose only -- to serve mankind. His service for us required the giving of His life. It is then clear, as we serve, we are giving our lives away for others.

The scriptures tell us to serve wholeheartedly. It means to serve with your heart, your soul, your mind, and your body. You do not withhold any part of your life from fully serving.

When you pour yourself wholeheartedly into everything you do for others, God will pour out His blessing, His favor and His abundance in your life.

Do I serve others with gladness?

____

____

____

____

____

The Power to Serve

So Jesus got up from the meal, took of His outer clothing, and wrapped a towel around His waist. After that, He poured water into a basin and began to wash His disciples' feet, drying them with the towel that was wrapped around Him.

John 13:4-5 (KJV)

Jesus demonstrated what service should look like. He did not consider serving His disciples or us as something that was beneath Him. He willingly gave His life for us by dying on the cross.

Jesus is the perfect example of servanthood. He gave and keeps on giving of Himself. In order for us to serve effectively, humility must be a foundation of our lives. Without humility, we will not be able to serve unselfishly.

When we choose to serve others, we set aside our own desires in order to meet the needs of others. Serving unselfishly is not a natural character trait. It takes perseverance and humility to submit our pride, ego, and needs so we can walk in someone else's shoes and make a difference in their life.

The power to serve comes though a relationship with Jesus Christ. He gives us the power and desire to say, "Yes, I am available and willing for whatever is needed from me."

The greatest key to serving is that you are not limited to a single position. You are at a place where God is molding you. When serving in Christ, you will always experience unspeakable joy.

Jesus is our perfect model of a servant, and we should follow His example and serve as He served.

Why is serving others so vital in my growth?

____

____

____

____

____

____

Heart of a Servant

Guard your heart above all else, for it is the source of life.

Proverb 4:23 (CSB)

Your heart is the center of who you are. It is from your heart that you gain the desire to serve. Whatever begins in your heart will affect your whole life. That is why you are encouraged in the scriptures to guard your heart.

It is from your heart that you serve not only God but also others. To have a heart of a servant, you must be committed to the things of God and to follow His plan for your life.

Each of us has been called to serve others, which means that we have a desire to make a difference. To serve others means that we have a desire to help people from all walks of life. As we serve, we must be courageous and not be afraid or ashamed to appear small in the eyes of the world to benefit the lives of people.

A person with a servant's heart gladly receives assignments, serves with a glad heart, and is willing to be led by the Holy Spirit of God, as they serve.

Some people in our society look down on those who clean or serve in restaurants or other service-related industries. They overlook the fact that many of these people are successful because they serve others and meet the needs of people.

It does not matter what your vocation is, as long as you are serving people in some way. What we must realize is that service is our highest calling, as it was for Jesus. He came to earth to save a needy people and went to the cross of Calvary because He was willing to serve us.

Jesus served us by dying! As you serve, you are becoming more and more like Jesus. Servanthood is a heat condition.

How do you know if you have the heart of a servant?

____

____

____

____

____

____

Requirements for Service

Therefore, I urge you, brothers, in view of God's mercy to offer your bodies as living sacrifices, holy and pleasing to God – this is your spiritual act of worship. Do not conform any longer to the pattern of this world, but be transformed by the renewing of your mind. Then you will be able to test and approve what God's will is, His good, pleasing and perfect will.

Romans 12:1-2 (NIV)

When we serve, there will be a requirement for fulfilling our service. One of the requirements is a willingness to offer ourselves to God, as an act of worship.

As we serve God, and do what He requires, other people may not be happy with our service to Him. As a result, we may spend more time than necessary trying to please people instead of pleasing God. You are required to please only Him! As you please Him, all others will eventually come in alignment with God.

The scriptures encourage us to consider others by putting them first. This is sacrificial giving when we willingly lay down our desires, and our lives to meet the needs of others.

We are required to give our all to be of service in the Kingdom of God. It is daily taking up our cross and following where God leads. This requires deep trust and confidence in God's ability to take care of us, as we serve Him and others.

Another requirement for service is to be faithful. A faithful person will grow and expand in the kingdom of God. God is looking for faithfulness in our service to Him and the people He places around us.

Are you faithful in your service to God?

____

____

____

Personal Notes/Reflection

Life Application:

1. Understand that service is your highest calling.
2. Service is your rightful position.

Chapter 8: Serve Generously

Ephesians 6:7-8 – Serve wholeheartedly, as if you were serving the Lord, not men, because you know that the Lord will reward everyone for whatever good he does, whether he is slave or free.

Service can either be viewed from a positive or negative mindset. Each time you serve with generosity you are planting seeds into good soil. When a seed enters the soil it will germinate, grow, and then bear fruit.

Each time you serve others you are planting seeds that will generate a harvest in your life. It is difficult to give you best seed and nor reap a harvest.

To serve generously, we must learn to give from our hearts. When we give from our hearts, it will benefit others and make a significant difference in their lives.

If we serve reluctantly - are we truly serving? Being joyful and cheerful in our services gives people an opportunity to see God at work in our lives. Each time we step out of self to serve others, God will cause His favor to abound in our lives.

When we serve with generosity, it is a demonstration of our heartfelt thanks to God for all He has done and will continue to do in our lives. When men see our generosity in serving others, they will know that it is God-inspired and God-given, which will enable them t praise God for His wonderful works.

As you serve, know that God will reward you for each act of service you provide.

Do I serve with generosity, or do I serve begrudgingly?

____

____

____

____

____

____

Wholehearted Service

And if you do good to those doing good to you, really of what credit is it to you? Even the sinners do the same.

Luke 6:33 (NWT)

When I consider wholehearted service, the word integrity and doing good comes to mind. Integrity is giving your all to whatever you have been called and chosen to do. It is the assurance others have that they can depend on you to keep your word. To wholeheartedly serve others, you must have total commitment to the process. This commitment must be such that, if you are unable to meet the obligation, you will call the person and state the reason that you are unavailable.

When you give to others you are serving the Lord wholeheartedly. All of your heart must become engaged and involved in your service so that the people you are serving will be blessed by your sacrifice.

You will face times of uncertainty as you begin to give your all in wholehearted service, but you must remember that courage will get you into position for God to use you and to bless you. It takes courage to do what seems impossible to you, but nothing is impossible with your God. If God has given you the assignment, He has also given you the grace to accomplish it.

God will not ask you to do something that He has not already equipped you to do. You may be unaware of the equipping; but as you take a step of faith - for some it will be a leap of faith, you will discover what you needed was already in you just waiting to be discovered.

What will it require for you to truly serve others as God has called you to?

____

____

____

____

____

____

The Sacrifice of Service

We put no stumbling block in anyone's path, so that our ministry will not be discredited. Rather, as servants of God we commend ourselves in every way: in great endurance; in troubles, hardships and distresses; in beatings, imprisonments and riots; in hard work, sleepless nights and hunger; in purity, understanding, patience and kindness; in the Holy Spirit and in sincere love.

II Corinthians 6:3-6 (NIV)

The Apostle Paul gives us a clear understanding of the cost that he and others endured, as they provided service to others for the cause of Christ. Hard work is a requirement for doing anything great either in the Kingdom of God or with your life.

All of you at times must sacrifice something, whether it is your time, efforts, or some friendships, as you pursue what God has destined for your life. I think about people who start new businesses. They spend countless hours both in the preparation process, as well as the time spent to provide the actual service. It costs them something to develop a successful business, but they were willing to make the sacrifice to meet the needs.

When you decide to do something of great value with your life, you must approach it with the understanding that this is a life-long commitment and responsibility. Often the preparation process will be labor-intensive, and you may have to endure some struggles to get to the end result. In this sacrifice, you must give total dedication to what you are doing in order for it to produce the results that you are seeking. At times you have to crucify your flesh and your personal desires to get to the desired destination. In any endeavor you consider pursuing, you have to prepare for disappointments.

What is my act of reasonable service to God?

____

____

____

____

____

____

The Reward of Service

And without faith it is impossible to please God, because anyone who comes to Him must believe that He exists and that He rewards those who earnestly seek Him.

Hebrews 11:6 (NIV)

There is a reward not only for your faith but also a reward for your service. Since God is the rewarder of those who seek after Him, He is also the rewarder of those who will provide service to others.

Your faith is the key that unlocks your storehouse of blessings, and that same faith brings pleasure to the heart of God. He is pleased with you, when you demonstrate confidence and trust in Him. You must believe that God exists in order for you to serve Him wholeheartedly.

At some point in your relationship with God, you must get beyond the point of just believing in Him, to a place of knowing that He is real and available to you. As you earnestly seek after Him, He comes with His rewards to your life. God is no respecter of persons. Wherever He finds faith, He rewards. God is looking for people who will demonstrate complete faith and confidence in Him.

If you take the principles of God's Word, embrace them, believe and apply them, they will work in your life even as God has allowed them to work in the lives of others. God is not partial. He will not bless one and not another who is applying the same principles of His Word in their life.

When you are faithful to God in your service to Him and others God will be doubly faithful to you. You cannot out give God so because you have given there is a great reward that awaits you. You must look for these rewards and expect them to daily unfold in your life.

Will my service to others be rewarded?

____

____

____

____

Hannah's Surrender to God's Service

And she was bitter of soul, and she began to pray to Jehovah and to weep greatly. And she went on to make a vow and say: O Jehovah of armies, if you will without fail look upon the affliction of your slave girl and actually remember me, and you will not forget your slave girl and actually give your salve girl a male offspring, I will give him to Jehovah all the days of his life, and no razor will come upon his head.

1 Samuel 1:10-11 (NWT)

Hannah was barren and could not have children so she went to God and beseeched Him for a son. God saw her heart and her desire; and because she was willing to surrender all to God, He gave her the desire of her heart – He gave her a son.

When Hannah pursued God, she received the reward of her pursuit and the answer to her prayers. I want you to take hold of this picture. The Bible said that for years she was mocked, scorned, and taunted. She wept and prayed for God to deliver her. God moved in her situation by rewarding her with a son. In turn, God used this longed-for son to be the Priest of the Israeli people. The son she sought God for earnestly, God used mightily.

Each time the people who knew her, when she was barren, heard the name "Samuel," they could not help but remember that this was Hannah's, the barren woman's, son. God not only gave her a son, but He gave her one that was famous, one who had His heart and was a leader in his nation.

Consider all the mothers who had children during Hannah's time. Their children have died and gone to their rewards, and today there is no mention of them in the Bible. However, the son Hannah prayed and waited for with such anguish has a different ending -- we are still hearing and learning about today. God is, indeed, a rewarder of those who diligently seek Him.

What is the deepest longing of your heart? God will also hear and answer you as He did Hannah, if you will not give up.

How can you serve generously?

____

____

____

____

____

____

Personal Notes/Reflection

Life Application:

1. Generosity comes from the heart.
2. You are called to serve others with generosity.

Chapter 9. The Pursuit of the Chosen

Hosea 1:2-3 (CSB) - When the Lord first spoke to Hosea, He said this to Him: "Go and marry a promiscuous wife and have children of promiscuity for the whole land has been promiscuous by abandoning the Lord." So he went and married Gomer daughter of Diblaim, and she conceived and bore him a son.

Hosea the prophet was known as the prophet of restoration, and his name means "Yahweh has saved." It is therefore not surprising that God would use His life to demonstrate to you His saving and redeeming grace.

The story of Hosea is a story of how God restores backsliders who have strayed away from Him. When I began to reflect on the pursuit of God, I could not help but be moved by the story of Hosea and the amazing love God has for us. Those whom God has chosen, He openly pursues with a tenderness and love that is measureless.

God is consistent in His pursuit even when time and time again we turn away from Him. He faithfully and consistently pursues us, as demonstrated by the command He gave Hosea to marry the prostitute.

The story of Hosea is a clear indication of the love of God for all His children. When God instructed Hosea to marry a temple prostitute, I can well imagine his reaction to God's command. It probably went something like this: "I know that I am not hearing from God. I am missing something here. What will my family and friends say about me? I will be the talk of the town because they will probably think that I have lost my mind."

Hosea did not hesitate to follow the instructions from God because He had a relationship with God and trusted his ability to hear and follow God's instructions.

There are times when God will ask all of us to do something out of the norm, and we must believe and move out based on what we hear God speaking to our hearts.

What has God asked me to do that does not appear normal?

____

____

____

____

____

Gomer

Hosea 1:3a – So he went and married Gomer daughter of Diblaim, and she conceived and bore him a son.

As I studied the life of Gomer, the prostitute, I could not help but wonder what devastation caused her to choose that life. In life you will go through many painful experiences; and, if you are not careful to find refuge in God, the enemy will cause you further devastation. I am sure that Gomer was wounded and needed to be rescued. God, in His infinite love, sent her a deliverer.

After marrying the prophet Hosea, God lifted Gomer from a life of pain, lack, and heartache and gave her a home and a family with someone well known throughout Israel. God took her from insignificance to a life of meaning and significance.

Many of us would have been content to stay there the rest of our lives, but not Gomer. It is clear that she had the love, the protection, and covering of a husband and home, yet she walked away and went back to a life of prostitution. With her decision, it is apparent that something vital was still missing in her soul and that her old nature had not been crucified. Gomer was still searching for something.

I am sure in her marriage to the Prophet she encountered many challenges from the Israeli people that she had to work at overcoming. Her self-worth and self-esteem had to be at the lowest level when dealing with the challenges and new responsibilities. She must have needed constant reassurance and encouragement. Even though God had rescued and redeemed her, she did not find her full sufficiency in Him and her family. There was a void that was still in her heart. Therefore, she went back to her former life looking for what she felt was still missing but not finding it. She only found a deeper level of pain and rejection and would once again require God to rescue and reclaim her.

How many times have God delivered us and we still find ourselves back in our old situations. The love of God will never stop pursuing you no matter what. He will keep pursuing you until He wins you back because His love for you is amazing.

What has God delivered me from and am I free indeed?

____

____

____

____

____

The Second Pursuit

Hosea 3:1 - Then the Lord sad to me, "Go again; show love to a woman who is loved by another man and is an adulteress, just as the Lord loves the Israelites though they turn to other gods and love raisin cakes.

After marrying the prophet and having three children, Gomer left her home and family and went back to prostitution. God told the prophet to go get her and to bring her home. Imagine with me how the prophet must have felt - his shame, embarrassment, and confusion over Gomer's desertion. He had given her his love, a home, and a family; but apparently, it was still not enough for her since she walked away from them.

God was not finished with Gomer or His pursuit of her. God instructed the prophet Hosea to go after her a second time and to bring her home. In obedience to God, Hosea went looking for her and found her not only back into prostitution, but that she was also sold into slavery. He purchased her for fifteen pieces of silver and five bushels of barley and took her home.

God allowed Hosea to experience this desertion by his wife to show him and the Israelites how their spiritual adultery grieved Him. God was showing them how it felt each time they walked away from Him.

In pursuing Gomer, God was demonstrating through the prophet the love He has for His people. He shows them that, even though they turn away from Him, He will not turn away from them. He continues to pursue us even when we have abandoned Him.

When we sin and completely miss God, He will faithfully, tenderly, and consistently come after us. He will receive us back into the fold, even after we have broken His heart with our wrong choices. When we return to Him, He is merciful and forgiving, never holding our sins and failures against us. He extends undeserved grace to us and never condemns us. When we return to Him, He simply says, “welcome home, my son, my daughter, welcome home.”

Like Gomer, many of us at times have walked away from God; but God keeps right on pursuing us. We are thankful to have such a loving and compassionate father.

How many times has God had to pursue you?

____

____

Personal Notes/Reflection

Life Application:

1. Believe that you are special to God.
2. You were created to be a giver just like God.

Chapter 10. The Quest

2 Chronicles 16:9a (NIV) - *For the eyes of the Lord range throughout the earth to strengthen those whose hearts are fully committed to Him.*

God is on a quest for you! He is on the lookout for you. He is searching for you because He wants to strengthen you. The eyes of God are roaming the earth, looking for people whose hearts are set on Him. He is looking for people who desire to please Him. In His search, God is looking for people with steadfast hearts -- hearts that are dedicated and committed to serve Him.

When God searches and finds these people, He chooses those that are sold out to His plans and purposes for their lives. In order to effectively fulfill the plans of God, you must be a mature believer in whom He can establish His covenant. If you are easily moved by every doctrine you hear, it will keep you from having a covenant relationship with God. I have known many people who have one foot in the Church and one in the world. The Bible defines them as being double-minded and easily blown away by every wind of doctrine.

God wants to raise a standard for all of you who are willing to serve Him with your whole heart. The standard is to stand for Him no matter what the cost.

The above scripture is clear that, when God finds these believers, He will strengthen them with His power and might so He can fulfill great destinies through them. It is, and has always been, the desire of God to bless you, to empower, and to give you access to everything in His Kingdom.

Do you know God is on a quest for you? Why?

____

____

____

____

____

Pursuing and Finding the Chosen

Matthew 12:18-21 (NIV) - Here is my servant whom I have chosen, the one I love in whom I delight; I will put My Spirit on him, and he will proclaim justice to the nations. He will not quarrel or cry out; no one will hear his voice in the streets. A bruised reed he will not break, and a smoldering wick he will not snuff out, till he leads justice to victory. In His name nations will put their hope.

The heart of God is tender and open toward you. He searches for His chosen people so He can love and show His delight in them. He wants to pour the essence of Himself into you so you can bring help to those in need. He is seeking for a people who will declare to nations His love, mercy, forgiveness, and hope.

When God gets hold of these people, He demonstrates an unchanging love toward them. He begins by showing them how much they please Him and bring joy to His heart. It is a picture of parents watching and observing everything that a newborn baby does. They are aware, alert, listening, watching, and engaging in every new accomplishment. They stand and applaud with delight and joy every victory and every step.

God is a loving parent who watches your every move and cheers you on. As you grow and develop, God begins to train you to maintain peace and order around you. He teaches you how to give compassion and mercy to those who need it. He teaches you to be like Him as you dispense to others the same grace He has given you.

In every difficult circumstance, God teaches you how to gain victory and how to keep the flame of hope alive in your heart. God is always pursuing you because He has chosen you for Himself.

Why does God pursue me?

____

____

____

____

____

Reasons for God's Pursuit

Jeremiah 1:5 (NIV) - Before I formed you in the womb I knew you, before you were born I set you apart; I appointed you as a prophet to the nations.

Have you ever chased after a job, relationship, or goal? In that chase were you committed and willing to do whatever was necessary to attain the prize? You prayed, you fasted, and sought wise counsel to ensure that you were in proper alignment so you would not miss the opportunity when it presented itself to you. You pursued the job, the relationship, or the goal because you knew that it would benefit your life and enrich you in many ways.

God has many reasons for His pursuit of you. Before you were conceived in the minds of your parents and even before your parents came together, God had already planned your life, your days, and your destiny. Before He selected the womb in which you would be born, He formed your personality and your character. He had intimate knowledge of who you were before you were born. It is clear that you existed in Him before your earthly parents even thought of you. He knew that some of you would have very direct and straightforward personalities while others would be quiet and calm.

We are created in the image of God, and the Bible says that God is a Spirit. It is, therefore, clear that our spirit was with God before He gave us a body to inhabit. When God formed us, He purposely set us apart and gave us various assignments to fulfill. He made us a prophet to the nations. We are the ones who will tell the truth of who He is to all those we meet. He gave us a voice so that we can testify of His goodness to all mankind.

As His prophets, we proclaim to the nations that there is no other God besides Him. We are His hands, feet, and voice to those who are in need of God's love, hope and grace.

Why has God chosen to pursue you?

Personal Notes/Reflection

Life Application:

1. Believe that you are special to God.
2. You were created to be a giver just like God.

Chapter 11. Preparation for Your Destiny

II Timothy 3:16-17 (CSB) - All Scripture is inspired by God and is profitable for teaching, for rebuking, for correcting, for training in righteousness, so that the man of God may be complete, equipped for every good work.

When most people hear the word "preparation," immediately a picture comes to mind - a picture of hard work or extra time spent in training. For others, it is a feeling of readiness and anticipation of a coming event.

Preparation is having foresight of a possible outcome. It is laying the groundwork for that which you desire to take place. Still for others it is preparing a solid foundation on which they can build a strong and secure destiny.

In Old Testament times, we find a clear picture of the world's definition of preparation. In Esther's time, a woman was presented to the king only after she had spent one year being purified and prepared. For six months, she was bathed in oils and myrrh to soften her skin. The next six months were spent applying all types of aromas and perfumes to her body. All bodily impurities had to be removed before she was presentable. The outer appearance had to be one of total perfection. Once the preparation process was complete, along with a host of other beautiful ladies, she was ready to be presented to the king who then made his choice.

Imagine spending a year being prodded, scrubbed, perfumed, and then finally meeting the king only to learn that he did not choose you. How disappointing that must have been for many of those young ladies and how devastating for others! In your life there is a season of preparation. This process is far different from the world's preparation process.

God is the one who prepares you for His purposes and plans and He is thorough in the process. The first step in the process is to come into an intimate and personal relationship with Jesus Christ. The moment you begin the relationship with Jesus, God begins preparing you for your destiny.

Am I currently being prepared for my destiny? How?

___

___

___

___

___

Our Acceptance

Luke 1: 38 – I am the Lord's slave, said Mary. "May it be done to me according to your word." Then the angel left her.

In order for us to be accepted by the King of Glory, our great God, the requirement is not one year of preparation or purification. We are acceptable just as we are, when we make Jesus our personal Savior and Lord. We find instant acceptance when we acknowledge that Jesus is the Son of God by believing that He was born of a virgin and willingly gave up His life on a cruel cross for us. When we acknowledge that He rose from the dead and is now seated at the right hand of God making intercession for us, we will find no rejection, only acceptance. To gain acceptance we must simply come to Him just as we are.

When the Holy Spirit begins to tug at our hearts, we make a decision to surrender our wills to Him; and He instantly comes in and begins a work of purification.

Jesus our Savior is not looking for outward perfection, but He is looking for hearts that are ripe and open to Him. He is looking for those who will say, "Yes, Lord." The moment you say "Yes" to Him, He comes in, and the transformation begins. Others can see the transforming work He does on the inside of you.

Like Mary the mother of Jesus who willingly said "Yes" to the plan of God for her life and our redemption, we must also willingly say "Yes" each time we hear the voice of God.

God is looking for a people who will not question Him regarding His plans and destinies for them but those who willingly undertake all that He assigns to their life to do.

Do you know and have you accepted God's call on your life?

____

____

____

____

Personal Notes/Reflection

Life Application:

1. Believe that you are special to God.
2. You were created to be a giver just like God.

Chapter 12. God's Preparation Process

John 15:1-8 (CSB) - I am the true vine, and My Father is the vineyard keeper. Every branch in Me that does not produce fruit He removes, and He prunes every branch that produces fruit so that it will produce more fruit. You are already clean because of the word I have spoken to you. Remain in Me, and I in you. Just as a branch is unable to produce fruit by itself unless it remains on the vine, so neither can you unless you remain in Me. I am the vine; you are the branches. The one who remains in Me and I in him produces much fruit, because you can do nothing without Me. If anyone does not remain in Me, he is thrown aside like a branch and he withers. They gather them, throw them into the fire, and they are burned. If you remain in Me and My words remain in you, ask whatever you want and it will be done for you. My Father is glorified by this: that you produce much fruit and prove to be My disciples.

It goes without saying that the preparation process of God is entirely different from ours. If you have been in relationship with God for any length of time, you will know that during His preparation He often goes after things in your life that are very deep and painful. He is after that which will cause you to grow and develop into the likeness of Christ.

Jesus makes it clear that He is the True Vine, our life source, and we are the branches who receive our nourishment from Him. He carefully watches over the branches to determine which ones are bearing fruit in His Kingdom. In order for the branch to bear any fruit, it must stay connected and reside within the source of life, the Vine.

As the Vine, Jesus is the stem of the plant, which gives support. He is the only one who can direct you to your destiny and support you in the fulfillment of it. The branch must abide with Jesus and act in accordance with His will to get the power it needs to be effective.

Part of abiding is that you not only agree with what Jesus says, but that you also submit to His plans. You are clearly depicted, as a branch, which means you are a part of the stem of the plant and not the plant itself, so you take your nourishment directly from Him.

Is God currently preparing you for destiny? How?

____

____

____

____

____

The Cleansing

I Peter 5:8 – Be sober, be on the alert! Your adversary the devil is prowling around like a roaring lion, looking for anyone he can devour.

Have you ever been at a place in your life when all seems well? For a change everything was going along peacefully. You found contentment and are happy to finally get there after much struggling. For a season, you continued to enjoy this contentment, then one day something happened that knocked you sideways, and you were plunged into a season of pain, hardship, and in some cases devastation.

The Bible is clear that the devil is like a roaring lion seeking whom he may devour (I Peter 5:8). It did not say he was a roaring lion but that he is like a roaring lion. I have seen pictures of lions without teeth and that is the picture of what the devil looks like. He seems tough and scary, but when he opens his mouth to roar at you, you realize to your amazement that he is toothless.

When you are plunged into seasons of pain and hurt, the toothless devil is roaring; and his roar can cause you some pain, as well as concern. God knows that the devil will roar into your life from time-to-time. His roar can be painful, but God will use the pain to begin His cleansing work in you. He begins to prune away things that seem perfectly fine and necessary to you.

I remember a time when I was finally in a season when I thought I was going to get some rest from my struggles and valleys. In the midst of this season, a friend decided to share some of my personal struggles with some of her friends. This friend had known me for a long time, and she knew I was a private person, yet she chose to share my personal information. This caused me great pain, and in the midst of my pain, I asked God why? His response was, "I am in the process of pruning unnecessary relationships out of your life so I can draw you closer to Me." I can truly say though, the pruning was as painful as it was necessary.

What is God currently pruning in my life?

____

____

____

Personal Notes/Reflection

Life Application:

1. Generosity comes from the heart.
2. You are called to serve others with generosity.

Chapter 13. Submission to the Process

I Peter 2:13-14 (NIV) - Submit yourselves for the Lord's sake to every authority instituted among men: whether to the king, as the supreme authority, or to governors, who are sent by Him to punish those who do wrong and to commend those who do right.

You serve an omniscient God who promised you eternal life from before time began (Titus 1:2). God knew that Adam would fail and implemented His plan for your redemption before the foundation of the world. I like to think that God the Father, God the Son, and God the Holy Spirit had a meeting in Heaven to determine which of them would redeem mankind.

One of them had to decide to be the perfect substitute for us. He had to yield up His title, be willing to be born as a baby, and suffer the hurt and pain of rejection in order to bring us eternal life.

The decision that Jesus made to be our Savior required the submission of His position, authority, and will to that of the Father. It took love and a willingness to die for others. In His submission, He accepted unjust punishment. When He was wrongfully accused, He did not in turn accuse others; and when He was threatened, He did not respond in kind.

He submitted to the preparation process because He understood what was at stake. We are told, "Who for the joy that was set before Him, endured the cross, despising the shame, and has sat down at the right hand of the throne of God" (Heb. 12:2). He willingly gave up His throne, splendor, worship, and adoration to save a people who would mock, ridicule, scorn, and then hang Him on the cross.

He submitted willingly, fully understanding what He would face. Jesus is our perfect example of submission - though right, He gave up His rights and went to the cross to redeem us.

How can I submit my life just like Jesus?

____

____

____

____

____

Our Submission

James 4:7 – Therefore, submit to God. But resist the devil and he will flee from you.

In order for you to totally submit, you must model yourself after the example of Jesus. You must acknowledge that submission is a part of the will of God for your life. You must first yield your will over to God with the full understanding that He will mold and shape you into the image and likeness of His Son.

As you begin submitting to the preparation process, the Bible encourages you to submit to one another -- to earthly authority, to men, to leaders, and to masters. To willingly submit yourself to these authorities, you should know that there is no loss of dignity; but there will be an increase in the power of God in your life.

Submission is not a subservient word or position. It takes a powerful person to truly submit to another's authority. Submission requires obedience even when you are not in full agreement. It is the total surrender of what you may think and believe to allow someone else the opportunity to be right. That takes power!

Have you ever been in a heated discussion, and you knew without a doubt that you were right, but in order to bring peace to the situation, you backed off? That is submission. Even though you were right, you yielded to another person's desire to be right in order to bring harmony. You give up your right to be right, and that decision has the power to transform your relationships and change the lives of the people who receive the benefit of your submission.

How can I experience the power in submission?

____

____

____

____

____

The Cost of Submission

II Timothy 2:15 (KJV) - Study to show yourselves approved unto God, a workman that needeth not to be ashamed, rightly dividing the word of truth.

To be successful in life you will often pay a price for your success. The preparation that is required for your success can come with a heavy price tag. This is not to scare you, but to let you know that you have to determine in your heart that you are prepared to go all the way with God so you can succeed.

You must determine that there is nothing too difficult that will prevent you from persevering till you attain your destiny. As I think back over the four years I spent in college, I can truly say that it was a great expense for me. Since I was responsible for the entire bill, I had to work; I found a job in a retail store. I went to class from seven in the morning to twelve noon on Mondays through Thursdays. I then worked from one in the afternoon to nine in the evenings. When I arrived home from work, I studied and prepared for the next day.

During that four-year period, I slept only five hours a night. Many of you can tell the same story. There was a cost, a sacrifice, to attain the things that you have thus far accomplished with your life. You willingly paid the price because you had a goal in mind. There is a cost to prepare yourself for what God has in store for you.

You have to be willing, available and flexible to what God has for you to do. You must be determined that no matter what the obstacles you will persevere because in persevering you will always win.

What am I willing to do to fulfill my destiny?

____

____

____

____

____

____

Time Commitment

Proverbs 6:10-11 - A little sleep, a little slumber, a little folding of the arms to rest, and your poverty will come like a robber; your need, like a bandit.

Your destiny requires time to plan and to prepare. In your time commitment, you should have seasons when you cannot be reached by phone. Often the phone keeps you distracted when you should be focusing on the task before you.

I cannot begin to tell you how often the phone would ring the moment I sat down to spend time with God or to begin working on a project that would lead to my destiny. I finally learned that ignoring it was not the key because the ringing would still disturb me. So I began turning it off during times of study and preparation so my mind and my heart could become focused on what was before me.

You have to decide how you will commit your time. Will you spend hours on the phone or in front of the television, when you have projects that need your attention?

The television is a distraction for many of you. You can spend hours of unproductive time watching it and living out other people's dreams instead of pursuing your own dreams.

You have to develop a schedule and a plan of action about how you will use your time. This will enable you to commit your time to that which will produce a harvest in your life.

In your time commitment, you will come to understand that nothing is as vital as the time you spend hearing from God and receiving the instructions He has for your life and the fulfillment of your destiny. Plan and prepare so you will not miss what God has for you.

What has been taking up the majority of my time?

____

____

____

____

____

____

Time Alone

1 Thessalonians 2:19 - 20 – For who is our hope, or joy, or crown of boasting in the presence of our Lord Jesus at His coming? Is it not you? For you are our glory and joy.

Each of you must have time alone to think and process the things that God is speaking to your spirit. This is time spent in the presence of God to ascertain what He has for you to do and to obtain a plan of action from Him.

In your "alone" time, you will pray, read the Word, and wait in the presence of God -- listening for His instructions. Each time you get before the Lord and petition Him, He will answer you.

You often miss hearing His answer because you do not wait long enough in His presence for Him to speak. You can become impatient, if He does not speak in the first two minutes and walk away without an answer from Him. I have been guilty of this and then wondered why God has not spoken to me. It is not that He has not spoken. It is that you are too busy to be still and hear His voice.

The Bible tells you that the Holy Spirit speaks in a still, small voice. He will not yell over the ringing of the phone, the noise of the television, or even the roar of normal conversations. I have not experienced many times in my life when the Holy Spirit has yelled or shouted to get my attention. The few times He has done so were to give me a warning of impending danger.

When God speaks to your heart, you need time to ponder and reflect on what you have heard and to wait for further instructions. A key to your success as you spend time alone with God is to know that His anointing is on the instructions that you hear, receive, and obey.

How often do I spend time alone with God?

____

____

____

____

____

Study Time

II Timothy 2:15 – Study to show thyself approved unto to God, a worker who do not need to be ashamed, correctly dividing the word of truth.

Second Timothy tells you to study to show yourself approved unto God. You study to develop an intimate relationship with God. You study to know Him and to understand His will and His ways. You study so you can be an imitator of Him and live the life He has destined for you.

As you study, you gain knowledge and are able to share that knowledge with others. When you know what God would do in any situation, you are able to pattern yourself after Him and give hope to others.

It has been said that people do not often listen to what is being said, but they watch what you do and model that. In this preparation season, you must study to demonstrate for others what God is revealing to you.

When you fill your heart with the Word of God and fill your mind with thoughts of Him, you can effectively share what you have learned with those He puts in your path.

You do not study to boast about what you know but to get to know God in all of His glory. You carve out time to study because you want to spend time with God and give Him pleasure. It is pleasing to God when you daily set time aside to spend with Him.

He has given you His Word so that you can study to know His will and plan for your destiny. Each time you open the pages of His Word, you encounter Him in a new and fresh way.

The Bible is alive and powerful and every word was designed to bring hope and healing to the believer. As you read and apply the principles that are contained in the Word of God, you are guaranteed a life of blessings, fullness, and prosperity.

Do I daily take time to study the Word of God?

____

____

____

____

The Sacrifice

Jonah 2:9 – But as for me, with the voice of thanksgiving I will sacrifice to you what I have vowed, I will pay. Salvation belongs to Jehovah.

The preparation season of your life will also require a sacrifice. The things you would readily do may have to be rescheduled. You will miss out on some fun activities because God is drawing you nearer to His Presence for further instructions.

You will sometimes have to sacrifice relationships. Some of your current friendships will not have the right ingredient to last in the next level of your destiny. You will have to leave some relationships behind because not everyone will understand your sacrifice, as you prepare.

Some people will tell you that it does not require "all that" to do what God has called you to do. They will not understand your dedication to the process or your willingness to give your time to it.

Others will not be able to understand, agree, or even comprehend your destiny and the plans you have to attain it. In the back of their minds, there will always be the thought that they knew you "back then." Since they have witnessed many of your mistakes and failures, they will not believe that God is speaking to you about the great destiny He has in store for you. If you are not careful, and do not have a willingness to let go of these relationships, you can become discouraged from pursuing God and His plans for you.

It truly requires a sacrifice to go all the way with God. It is called a living sacrifice.

How willing are you to sacrifice what is necessary to fulfill your destiny?

____

____

____

____

____

Living Sacrifice

Romans 12:1 – Therefore, brothers, by the mercies of God, I urge you to present your bodies as a living sacrifice, holy and pleasing to God; this is your spiritual act of worship.

To present a living sacrifice of our lives to God means that we willingly give Him all that we are in exchange for all that He is. It also means that we can no longer gratify our flesh with what we say and do. We must subject our flesh to the guidance of the Holy Spirit who lives in us.

Our spirits were created to have control over our entire life. The flesh was not designed to rule us, but because of sin many of us are controlled by our fleshly desires.

In the preparation process, you learn how to subject your flesh to your spirit by doing what is necessary and required. Preparation causes you to suppress what you would normally do so you can accomplish what is set before you.

Each time you say "No" to the flesh and its desires, you are saying "Yes" to God and His will for you. As you sacrifice time on the phone, watching the television, and letting go of some unhealthy relationships so you can draw nearer to God, He will draw near to you and fill you with more of Himself.

There is a sacrifice for everything that is worth attaining and it requires dying to self. When we get 'self' out of the way, God then has clearance to work in us and through us, as He desires.

Make it your prayer that the Lord will teach you how to crucify your flesh so your spirit can rule and govern every single decision that you make.

Am I willing to offer my life to God as a living sacrifice?

____

____

____

____

____

Personal Notes/Reflection

Life Application:

1. Generosity comes from the heart.
2. You are called to serve others with generosity.

Chapter 14: The Need for Preparation

II Timothy 3:17 (NIV) - So that the man of God may be thoroughly equipped for every good work.

During the early years of my life, my grandmother, Elizabeth, taught me about the need for preparation. She not only taught me how to prepare for life, but she taught me what was needed and necessary in the preparation process.

The first thing she revealed to me that required preparation was my need for a Savior in the form of Jesus Christ. From an early age she took me to church but did not push me to accept Christ. She regularly prayed and prepared the way for me to encounter Him.

When I gave my heart to the Lord, at the age of twelve, she was the first to share it with the family. I must say that many of my family members told me that I was too young, and it would not stick. I am here to tell you that I was not too young, and I have been saved for many years because my grandmother prepared me to encounter my Savior.

Each of you must prepare those you love to encounter the Savior no matter how young they are. God begins to work on the hearts of His children from an early age so they will not miss any time in their relationship with Him.

Each night my grandmother helped me prepare my attire for the next school day, and each morning she prepared breakfast and lunch for me. In all of this, my grandmother recognized and fulfilled a need in me. She equipped me with what I needed to ensure that I produced good work. You were born with a need to prepare for life, your future, and your destiny.

Do you understand that preparation is a must for your destiny?

____

____

____

____

____

Reasons for Preparation

II Timothy 2:24-25 (NIV) - The Lord's servant must not quarrel; instead, he must be kind to everyone, able to teach, not resentful. Those who oppose him, he must gently instruct, in the hope that God will grant them repentance leading them to the knowledge of the truth.

Here Paul clearly states to Timothy what it means to serve the Lord. You serve the Lord when you serve others. In His service, you prepare yourself to be kind, gentle, and teachable as He instructs you to lead His people. If you are unprepared, you will fail when you encounter people who try your patience and are unwilling to be taught.

The preparation process enables you to stand when you face trials. It is clear in the above passage of scripture that time spent with God in preparation will empower you to take care of the needs of others.

In God's preparation, you learn to put away the desire to be quarrelsome, when you are not getting your own way. In your daily service to God, you will encounter people whom you might feel are not reachable and are unapproachable. In these encounters, you must have gentleness, as you instruct them in the things of God. You must ask for God's help and guidance so you can direct the people to Him. As you direct them to God, and they come to a place of repentance, God will reveal His love and truth to them.

You prepare so that you will be successful in the assignments that God gives to you. The preparation process stabilizes you so that you can build a strong and solid foundation on which you can establish something that is lasting.

What keeps me from preparing?

____

____

____

____

____

Genesis 3:1 – Now the serpent was the most cunning of all the wild animals that the Lord God had made. He said to the woman, "Did God really say, 'You can't eat from any tree in the garden'?"

There is a permissive will of God and a perfect will of God. Many Christians live in the permissive will of God but not in His perfect will for their lives. In His permissive will, God will allow you certain things you ask for even though it may not be in His best plan for your life. In this permissive will, you are given permission to make some of your own choices.

Often you obtain permission because you have nagged, begged, and pleaded with God so often that He simply turns it over to you -- to do as you will. Many of you make your choices in disobedience to what He has told you to do. He allows you the choice to use your own will and intellect to make your decision. He does so because He knows that each decision and each choice will provide a lesson in your life, often a painful lesson, which will help you in your growth and development.

Consider the story of Adam and Eve. God gave them permission to eat off every tree in the garden except one, but they disobeyed Him and ate from the very tree He told them not to.

God was neither asleep nor unaware, when they made their choice. He knew exactly where they were and what they were about to do, and He could have stopped them at anytime by overriding their will. Since He created them with a free will, this gave them the ability to choose, and they chose to disobey Him. This was not the perfect plan of God for them or for the human race, but He had to abide by their decision.

God will also abide by your decision though His desire is that you choose His will over yours.

Am I operating in the permissive will or in the perfect will of God?

____

____

____

____

____

The Perfect Will of God

Galatians 2:19b-20 – I have been crucified with Christ; and I no longer live, but Christ lives in me. The life I now live in the flesh, I live by faith in the Son of God, who loved me and gave Himself for me.

In the perfect will of God you receive His instructions. Unlike Adam and Eve, you choose to do things His way -- you do not disobey Him but obey His commands.

You learn to listen, hear, and obey the instructions of the Holy Spirit, when He speaks to your heart. When you hear Him, you submit your will over to Him and do what He tells you to do. You accept that God is in full control, and you give way to whatever He wants to do.

In His perfect will for you, it is no longer you that lives, but Christ living through you (Gal. 2:20). In His will, you listen by engaging your mind, heart, ears, eyes, and your entire being on what God is saying and doing.

When you hear Him, you do exactly what you are told by following His instructions. You then obey what you hear by actively engaging yourself with God and allowing Him to become fully engaged with you, in you, and through you. To obey Him means that you follow His plan, do what He tells you to, and come to an understanding that He knows what is best for you. You blindly follow where He leads because you know He will never lead you down the wrong path for your life nor will He ever fail you.

In this preparation process, you will also learn that it is and always has been the plan of God to increase you and take you from glory to glory in Him. Therefore, choose to make God a daily part of your agenda by scheduling time to meet with Him face-to-face.

Am I living in God's perfect will for my life? Explain

____

____

____

____

____

Personal Notes/Reflection

Life Application:

1. Generosity comes from the heart.
2. You are called to serve others with generosity.

Chapter 15: Fulfilling Your Destiny

Joshua 1:2-3 (CSB) - Moses my servant is dead. Now you and all the people prepare to cross over the Jordan to the land I am giving the Israelites. I have given you every place where the sole of your foot treads, just as I promised Moses.

All of you, at one time or another have felt an urgency to accomplish something with your life. Coupled with these feelings is a desire to know why you were born and why you are here. These devotionals are designed to give you some signs to look for in the process of discovering your destiny.

Now, let us embark on the journey to discover how you can fulfill your destiny. Fulfillment comes in many different forms. Some of you are fulfilled with a good-paying job, a good family life, money in the bank, and a nice home; but then there are others who have a desire for more. It is important to know that God has designed each of you differently, and each one must discover what will bring ultimate fulfillment.

In your search to discover what fulfills you, do not compare your satisfaction level with someone else. To be fulfilled is to be satisfied with what you have and where you are in your life. It is a feeling of contentment when you have realized or fulfilled a dream or a goal. This feeling of gratification comes when you learn to rest in the promises of God, take what He says about you to heart, and then apply it to your own life. The fulfillment you experience in your life and in your walk with Him ensures that you are prepared and equipped not only to discover but also to fulfill your destiny.

God will be fully involved in the fulfillment of your destiny.

How will I fulfill my destiny?

____

____

____

____

____

____

Abraham's Journey to His Destiny

Genesis 12:1-4 (NIV) - The Lord had said to Abram, "Leave your country, your people and your father's household and go to the land I will show you. I will make you into a great nation and I will bless you; I will make your name great, and you will be a blessing. I will bless those who bless you, and whoever curses you I will curse; and all peoples on earth will be blessed through you." So Abram left, as the Lord had told him; and Lot went with him. Abram was seventy-five years old when he set out from Haran.

In Chapter I, we discovered that Abraham was willing to obey and follow God in the fulfillment of his destiny. When he left his homeland and began his walk in fulfilling His destiny, he chose separation from all that was familiar to him. He believed a voice, which he could not see, to be the voice of the true and living God; and he put action to his belief and began pursuing God for further instructions and directions.

As an acknowledgement that he heard and that he would obey the instructions, Abraham built an altar where God spoke to him. He memorialized the place by setting up a monument. This monument was a reminder to him about when and where God spoke, and that God would be faithful to do what He said.

Abraham traveled throughout the land looking for the right place to begin his purpose. He ended up in Egypt because there was a famine in the land of Canaan. He did not yet fully understand that God was His source, and that God could provide for him even in the midst of famine.

God allowed Abraham to journey to Egypt because it would become the place of testing and preparation for his destiny. Abraham was tested and failed in a number of his tests, but God did not abandon him. God continued to walk with him until he arrived at the right destination.

God will also be with you even when you have not passed all your tests on the way to your destination. He will never leave you but will guide you each step of the way.

What tests have you failed on the way to your destination?

____

____

____

____

____

____

Joseph's Journey to His Destiny

Genesis – 37:5 – Then Joseph had a dream. When he told it to his brothers, they hated him even more.

Joseph's brothers sold him into slavery, and he ended up in Egypt in Potiphar's house. Joseph found himself alone and in a strange country with no one to depend on but God for support, encouragement, and direction because of his isolation. Joseph was at a place in his life where he had to depend and rely totally on God.

This season in his life would develop a deeper and more abiding relationship with God. God would become his refuge, his confidant, and the only one who would hear his cry and grant him deliverance. In his journey, Joseph encountered times of testing that would equip him for the destiny God had selected him to fulfill.

His first test came in the form of Potiphar's wife who tried to seduce him while he was a servant in his master's house. This first test was a *flesh test.* In this test, God allowed Joseph to be tempted so that Joseph could see what was in his heart. When he faced this test, he told Potiphar's wife that he would not sin against his God. I want you to notice that Joseph's focus was on God, and he was determined to do nothing that would be a stain on God's name.

His next test was a *position test.* In this test, Joseph found himself in prison serving thirteen years for a crime he did not commit. Prison was a place of hardship and lack for a young man who was beloved and favored at home. Joseph, in this lowly position, continued to trust God and to serve Him with all of his heart. He did not have an attitude because he was demoted but served where he was planted.

What is your attitude when you are demoted or not appreciated?

____

____

____

____

____

Journey to Your Destiny

Exodus 23:20 (CSB) - I am going to send an Angel before you to protect you on the way and bring you to the place I have prepared.

It is exciting and encouraging to know that God does not expect you to discover your destiny on your own. He has put a plan in place to get you to your place of destiny.

In His Kingdom, angels are assigned to do what God bids them to. In the above passage of scripture, God makes it clear that He will send angels before you to protect and bring you safely to the place He has prepared for you.

As believers, angels have been assigned to us, the heirs of salvation. They are assigned to guard, protect, help, and watch over us to ensure that we do not come to harm. As you begin the journey to your destination, keep in mind that God has already prepared the place that He has for you.

He has gone before you to annihilate any enemies that would hinder you from taking rightful occupancy of your promised land.

Just recall the story of the children of Israel's journey out of captivity. As God delivered them from Egyptian bondage and sent them on a journey to their promised land, a place flowing with milk and honey, He sent terror and confusion ahead of them to route the inhabitants of the land that they were to occupy. Angels were sent before them to prepare the way and to fight for you. Angels have gone before you as well and they are at work preparing your place of destiny.

Are you aware that angels have been assigned to you?

____

____

____

____

____

____

Personal Notes/Reflection

Life Application:

1. Generosity comes from the heart.
2. You are called to serve others with generosity.

Chapter 16: Hindrances to Fulfilling Your Destiny

I Thessalonians 2:18 (NIV) - For we wanted to come to you certainly I, Paul, did, again and again but Satan stopped us.

You have all encountered times when you have been hindered from getting something you truly wanted. On the journey to your destiny, many of you will encounter hindrances that are designed to discourage you from the pursuit.

You have to recognize these hindrances and allow God to show you how to overcome them. It is the enemy's job to discourage and to keep you from moving forward, but it is your job to resist him and overcome all of the tactics he places in your path on the way to your destiny.

He is on an outright attack to keep the blessings of God from flowing into your life. When he tries his best to hinder you, remember that the greater One lives in you and He gives you the power to overcome in every situation.

You must tap into the power source, which is the Holy Spirit, so that you can withstand any attempt of the enemy to keep you in mediocrity and away from your destination. God's plans for your life are marvelous and He desires that you experience all He has for you. Do not let the enemy keep you from attaining these great plans for your life.

What has been hindering me from fulfilling my destiny?

____

____

____

____

___

___

___

Doubt

Mark 11:22-24 (NIV) - "Have faith in God," Jesus answered. "I tell you the truth, if anyone say to this mountain, 'Go, throw yourself into the sea,' and does not doubt in his heart but believes that what he says will happen, it will be done for him. Therefore I tell you, whatever you ask for in prayer, believe that you have received it and it will be yours."

One of the greatest tools of the enemy to keep you from the destiny, which God has reserved for you, is doubt. Doubt keeps you from hearing clearly and from moving in any direction.

Doubt can be crippling to the degree that you are afraid to move toward your goals. When you doubt, you are unable to hear instructions from God clearly and can develop a lack of confidence in His ability to help you.

In your doubt, you do not expect anything good to happen to you. You often expect the worst in the situations of your life. Doubt is a heart condition. It keeps you from believing that anything is possible. If you cannot see or understand that all things are possible to those who believe God, then you are unable to dream and to accomplish those dreams.

Doubt causes your view to be cloudy and you cannot get a clear picture of what you need. When you are in doubt, you are unsure of yourself and not able to make right decisions or any decision at all. In your doubting, you often wonder if God cares about you and whether He will answer when you call to Him.

Doubting God is not a proper position for any of His children because He has proven time and again how faithful He is.

What causes you to doubt God?

____

____

____

____

____

Unbelief

Matthew 13:57 - 59 – And they were offended by Him. But Jesus said to them, "A prophet is not without honor except in his hometown and in his household." And He did not do many miracles there because of their unbelief.

Have you ever experienced times when you wondered if God was really there and whether He heard as you called to Him?

While teaching a recent Bible study, I asked the attendees what was keeping them from a consistent prayer life. The response from most of them was that they were unsure as to whether God was hearing them or not. Because of their unbelief, they could not commit to consistency in prayer. This lack of consistency was keeping them from getting to the best plan of God for their lives.

Unbelief can be damaging to your relationship with God because you think that many of the things He desires to give you are too far-fetched and unbelievable. As you battle unbelief, you can be skeptical in your outlook on life and doubt what you may be able to accomplish. Your unbelief will keep you from obtaining anything of great value. God designed you with the ability to believe and trust Him.

From an early age, most of you learned to trust your parents, have confidence in what they said, and in their ability to provide and take care of you. God is your Father and He desires that you have the same level of belief and trust in His ability to hear and provide for you. When you lack belief, you are literally saying to God, "You are not big enough or great enough to handle the things that are a problem for me." Imagine telling that to our big, awesome and amazing God.

What is your level of belief in God?

____

____

____

____

____

____

____

Fear

II Timothy 1:7 (NKJV) - For God has not given us a spirit of fear, but of power and of love and of a sound mind.

Fear is a spirit and it did not come from God. God has not given you the spirit of fear but of faith in Him and His ability.

The devil uses fear to keep many of you out of your Promised Land. He used it on the Israelites when they saw giants in the Promised Land that God gave them. Fear kept them from entering in.

Today his plan of attack has not changed. He is still using fear to intimidate many of you. God has not given you the spirit of fear, but of power, love, and a sound mind. God has given you His power to overcome and annihilate fear.

The love that you have for God and others will flush fear out of your life. Many of you have a fear of failure. You must look at the fear of failure in a different light. A failure is not failure, but only an opportunity to learn. When you and I fail at a project, it is a great opportunity to learn what could have been done differently. This failure brings you closer to success because you are able to put that failed attempt, the thing that did not work, behind you.

In order for you to stop fearing failure, you must know that when you fail you are not a failure. You should not take it personally. You simply failed in your attempt at what you were trying to do, but you yourself are not a failure. You are only a failure when you refuse to try and to step out in faith.

Do you know that it is impossible for you to fail because the Holy Spirit lives in you?

____

____

____

____

____

____

____

Knowledge/Education

1 Timothy 2:15 – Study to show thyself approved unto God, a workman that needeth not to be ashamed, rightly dividing the word of truth.

While I was teaching a message recently, I had a revelation that not many men and women in the Bible were college-educated! This revelation came to light because many of you put limitations on your abilities and yourself. You limit yourself by thinking about what you can and cannot accomplish due to your lack of education and knowledge.

God does not qualify or disqualify you because of your education level. He is not looking at what earthly man is looking for when they hire or promote you. God looks at your heart to see if you are trustworthy and can be useable to Him. Some of you have used your lack of knowledge and lack of education as a hindrance to keep you from moving forward.

When God called and chose you, He qualified you to fulfill greatness with your life. He has pre-wired you with everything you need to succeed. You are handpicked and qualified for the task that has been assigned to you. Though you may feel limited in your abilities, God has not limited you because of those abilities. I heard these words from a song long ago, which simply say, "If You can use anything, Lord, You can use me." The qualification to be useable is to say, "Yes, Lord," and to surrender your will and your plans over to God. In surrendering, you are saying to God, "I trust your preparation, and I will be open to however you want to use me to bring glory to your name."

When God called you to this great destiny, He knew He would have to qualify and prepare you to feel worthy enough so you would embrace what He has in mind for you. Part of this qualification came when you said, "Yes" to Him. With the indwelling presence of the Holy Spirit, you are thoroughly equipped to fulfill every good work.

How am I spending time with God so He can use me for His purpose?

____

____

____

____

____

Outside Influences

Romans 13:8 – Do not you people be owing anybody a single thing, except to love one another; for he that loves his fellowman has fulfilled the law.

You can be hindered and stopped by the influences of others. Many times, you will encounter people, including family and friends, who do not believe that you are truly hearing from God because of the greatness of the destiny He is revealing to you. These outside influences can keep you from obtaining your destiny because of their belief system. If they do not believe that you are hearing from God, they can deposit their doubt in you and cause you to question whether you are truly hearing God.

Many of you will walk away from your destiny because you do not have the support of your family and friends. You believe if they cannot see the greatness of your destiny, no one else will. That is a lie from the enemy. Most of the time, the people that are closest to you are unable to clearly see because of their foreknowledge of you.

You cannot base your entire destiny on what people think or say because you will miss out on great opportunities every time. Give them the respect of hearing them out but do what the older generation says: "grind your own meal." Make your own decision. In the final analysis, God is the only one who knows what you have been equipped to accomplish since He did the equipping. The only thing He asks of you is to love one another.

You can trust that He will not lead you astray but will only lead you down the best path for your life. He is the only influence that you must truly consider. Trust the work He has faithfully begun in you and know that He will not stop until it is fully accomplished. Hear the counsel of your family and friends; but decide that you will base your final decision on the wisest counsel of all, the counsel of the Holy Spirit of God.

Who is influencing your belief about what God has spoken to you?

____

____

____

____

____

Personal Notes/Reflection

Life Application:

1. Generosity comes from the heart.
2. You are called to serve others with generosity.

Chapter 17: Five Steps to Your Destiny

Psalm 37:23 (CSB) - A man's steps are established by the Lord, and He takes pleasure in his way.

As I reflect on the reasons God would plan such great destinies for us, I cannot help but think of His great love for us. Because He so loved us He gave us His very best in the form of His Son. God adores the people He created, and because you are His, there is nothing good that He will ever withhold from you.

God is your Abba, He is your Father, and for many of you that is enough, but there are others of you who know Him as Daddy, the One who has been there and has been faithful to you every step of the way. You have intimate knowledge of your Daddy, and He has intimate knowledge of you because you have spent time with Him learning to walk in His footsteps.

God is ordering your steps to the special life He has planned for you who fear and reverence Him. He will fulfill the desires of all who stand in awe of His great goodness. He is a protective Daddy who watches over every step you take, to keep you from stumbling and falling. If you stumble and fall, He is right there to pick you up and set you on the right path again.

As you get in step with God, He will bring the blessings and greatness from His Kingdom into your life. These blessings were designed to bring fullness into your life. When you seek God, and not His blessings, He will pour all of His substance into you. The very blessings you long for will be a part of the deposit you receive from Him, as He takes up residency in your life

What is my true relationship with God?

____

____

____

____

____

Intimacy with God

Philippians 3:10 (NIV) - I want to know Christ and the power of His resurrection and the fellowship of sharing in His sufferings, becoming like Him in His death.

To get in step with God you must have an intimate relationship with Him. In this intimate relationship, you accept Him as your Savior and begin a life of service to Him.

There are many people who know Jesus as Savior, but not as Lord. When you accepted Jesus, He came into your life, and you now know that when you die you will spend eternity with Him. There are some people, however, who know Him not only as Savior but also as Lord. These people have made the decision that they want more than to just spend eternity with God; they desire to know Him in a more intimate way.

To know Him intimately they have submitted and surrendered their entire life to Him. He helps them with every decision whether small or great, and they do not make a move without consulting Him. He has clearance to tell them what to do, when to do it, and how to do it. They wait for His okay before moving forward. In their surrendering, they have given everything totally over to His control so He can use them as He desires. The hand of God touches every part of their lives. His signature is on everything they do. When you see them, you see a reflection of God because God is the captain of their souls and the master of their ship.

This level of intimacy requires a willingness to submit all that you are and ever will be to the care of a loving God. Someone defined intimacy as "into me see." God sees your heart and blesses you because He is faithful.

What is the level of your intimacy with God?

____

____

____

____

____

Obedience

I Samuel 15:22 (CSB) - Then Samuel said: Does the Lord take pleasure in burnt offerings and sacrifices as much as in obeying the Lord? Look: to obey is better than sacrifice; to pay attention is better than the fat of rams.

Everyone has struggled with obedience. Some of you struggled to obey your parents as you were growing up. I am sure that at times you struggled to obey and submit to instructions from your boss. Many of you have struggled with doing what is right and good.

It seems that there is a war going on in you when you decide to obey and do the things that you are called to do. God does not take pleasure in the things you do or the sacrifices you make. What pleases God is your obedience to Him and doing what He has instructed you to do.

The steps of obedience will lead you into a fulfilling destiny, while the steps of disobedience will keep you living below your privileges. To get to any level in God you must learn to hear and obey His instructions.

As a young adult, I learned a song which went something like this, "Trust and obey, for there is no other way to be happy in Jesus; you must trust and obey." In order for you to experience happiness and fulfillment, you must first learn to hear, trust, and obey the voice of God.

Am I obeying God's instructions for my life?

____

____

____

____

____

Faith/ Confidence

Hebrews 11:1 (CSB) - Now faith is the reality of what is hoped for, the proof of what is not seen.

Our faith pleases God. In fact, it is impossible to please God without having faith and confidence in Him. In your walk toward your destination, you must not only clothe yourself with humility, but you must also clothe yourself with faith.

Faith is the armor, which ensures that you annihilate the attacks of the enemy against you. Faith moves and activates God to go to work on your behalf, and it is the substance that will get you to your destiny.

Your faith must be solid and secure in what God has spoken to you about your life. Without absolute confidence in His word and ability, you will not enjoy the richness of your destination. Without faith, many of you merely exist from day to day. Faith gives meaning and life to your existence.

To activate your faith and receive your rewards you must speak what God has already spoken about you. When you begin to speak His Word back to Him, you activate your faith by kicking it into gear, which brings it roaring to life.

In your destiny, you must put action to what you believe. Every act of faith requires movement in the direction of the things for which you believe. You have a *voice of faith,* which activates your faith as it is used to petition God for the fulfillment of your destiny. Without consistency in speaking God's Word about yourself, you will not experience great success.

What is my level of faith in God?

____

____

____

____

Commitment

I Corinthians 15:58 (KJV) - Therefore, my beloved brethren, be ye steadfast, unmovable, always abounding in the work of the Lord, forasmuch as you know that your labor is not in vain in the Lord.

Commitment is the glue that keeps you steadfast at your faith address. It ensures that you are not moved regardless of what you hear or see. Commitment is your pledge to God and yourself about what you are contracting and promising to do. Commitment in its simplest form is to do what you say. It is to be entrusted with responsibilities and to have a determination to fulfill them.

Your level of commitment is determined by your love for God and your love for what He has called you to do. The level of your confidence in what you hear God saying will also determine your ultimate commitment. This commitment in the preparation process will keep you from straying away from the faith and make you fully available for the highest level of service.

Commitment keeps you in the character-building process. It dares to ask the questions, "Are you a person of your word?" and "Do you follow through?" Your character is in a perpetual development cycle based on the commitments you keep. Your words will shape your life and define who you are. People assess your character as you honor your commitment.

Each time you make a commitment and keep it, you die to self by putting others first. In your commitment to God, you are willing to sacrifice in order to help others and to allow God to stretch you so that you can grow and develop into the person He birthed you to be.

What is the level of my commitment to God and myself?

____

____

____

____

____

Time in the Waiting Room

Isaiah 40:31 (KJV) - But they that wait upon the Lord shall renew their strength; they shall mount up with wings as eagles; they shall run, and not be weary; and they shall walk, and not faint.

Have you ever spent time in a hospital waiting room? I have and it can be an unsettling and sometimes traumatic event. For many it is a time of worry, a time of praying, and a time of hoping for a good report.

During my Christian walk, I have discovered that we will spend much time in the waiting rooms of life. In these waiting rooms, God continues the process of making you into the image of His Son. Time spent in the waiting room fashions you to be of service in the Kingdom.

The waiting room is a place where God begins to do a deep work in you to prepare you for your destiny. It is a time of purging and cleansing to make you fit and useable by the Master. The waiting room causes your fleshly will and desires to be crucified so that you can embrace His will and desires. As you struggle and wait, you truly learn dependency on God. You learn to trust Him fully for everything by understanding that only He can give you a breakthrough.

Whatever is unnecessary in your life will be stripped away in the waiting room. God uses this time to trim excess fat and baggage from your life. This time is Throne time alone with God. This is a time when God purges, cleanses, and purifies you for further use in His kingdom.

Are you currently waiting on God to move in your life?

____

____

____

____

____

Personal Notes/Reflection

Life Application:

1. Generosity comes from the heart.
2. You are called to serve others with generosity.

Chapter 18: Living in the Rewards and Blessings of Your Destiny

Hebrews 11:6 (CSB) - Now without faith it is impossible to please God, for the one who draws near to Him must believe that He exists and rewards those who seek Him.

It will take faith to get to your destiny just as it did for Abraham and Joseph to walk into the fulfillment of their destinies and enjoy what God had reserved for them.

When God finally walked them to their destination, it was beyond anything they could image or dream. They were blessed with abundance in their family life, in their spiritual walk, and in their finances. They were spiritually wealthy because they learned total dependence on God. God made their names great throughout the land. They had prominence, they were influential leaders, and they are still highly regarded even today.

Joseph never experienced that degree of loss or lack in his life again. Abraham, through his son Isaac, had children as numerous as the sand on the seashore and the stars in the sky, just as God promised.

Abraham became the father of nations and of our faith. Even, his son, Ishmael, who was not the promised heir, prospered and became extremely wealthy just because he was Abraham's seed.

Though the journey to their destiny was paved with difficulties, hardship, lack, and loneliness, they did not stop moving forward. They believed, they trusted, they waited, and then they walked into a promised land overflowing with all the goodness of God.

What are your rewards in your destiny?

____

____

____

____

____

The Reward of Peace

Philippians 4:6-7 (CSB) - Don't worry about anything, but in everything, through prayer and petition with thanksgiving, let your requests be made known to God. And the peace of God, which surpasses every thought, will guard your hearts and your minds in Christ Jesus.

Without peace, you will not be able to enjoy the rewards and blessings you receive from God. It takes the peace of God to keep your mind stable and your heart open to receive.

A lack of His peace produces anxiety and fear in your heart and mind. These things rob you of the enjoyment of your blessings. When your heart and mind are crowded with cares, it keeps you from finding true rest and hope in a loving and caring God.

It is His desire to give you the Kingdom, and in doing so, He wants you to enjoy all the benefits that come with Kingdom living. In His Kingdom, He fills your heart with His perfect peace, and you find rest for your soul under the shelter of His protection.

As you find peace, you live in divine health and prosper in whatever you put your hands to. To ensure you receive and enjoy your rewards, God has provided for your physical health and wealth. Your health starts first with the peace that guards your heart and mind through Christ Jesus. If your mind is healthy and whole, your body will follow suit.

Are you enjoying a life of peace?

____

____

____

____

____

____

Spiritual Wealth

III John 1:2 (NKJV) - Beloved, I pray that you may prosper in all things and be in health, just as your soul prospers.

Spiritual wealth is the level of intimacy you have with the Lord, which also brings about soul prosperity. When you spend time cultivating a relationship with Him, He enriches your life with His many provisions.

Spiritual wealth is unlimited to those who desire to have it. The more you pursue God, the more He will fill you to overflowing with a wealth of wisdom, knowledge, and grace. Each day, as you walk into His Presence, will be a day you are bestowed with new mercies. You will never truly spend time with God and come away dry or empty-handed. It is impossible.

God welcomes you with open arms and lots of joy when you seek after Him. The spiritual wealth you receive as part of your reward and blessing will flood your life with hope, courage, and faith to reach out and grab hold of the goodness of our God.

As God rewards you by filling you with Himself, you will begin to look like Him, walk like Him and talk like Him. When people see you, they will see a reflection of His glory and majesty. This reflection will draw them to you so you can direct them to the Light.

Are you living a life crowned with spiritual wealth?

____

____

Financial Wealth

Proverbs 13:22 (KJV) - A good man leaveth an inheritance to his children's children: and the wealth of the sinner is laid up for the just.

Job 36:11 (NIV) - If they obey and serve Him, they will spend the rest of their days in prosperity and their years in contentment.

The above scriptures and many others throughout the Bible make it abundantly clear that God wants you to have wealth and financial blessings. In order for you to leave an inheritance to your grandchildren, you must have a financial portfolio.

God fully intends for you to be blessed financially, to be a blessing to your family, and to have enough left over to give to those in need. He goes on to tell you that the wealth of sinners is laid up and set aside for you who are just.

When you obey and serve Him, your days will be filled with rest, prosperity, and contentment and He will bring you to your wealthy place. He gives seed to the sower so you can sow into the lives of people who are experiencing financial difficulties. He said, "He who is kind to the poor lends to the Lord, and He will reward him for what he has done" (Prov. 19:17).

You must have something to give to the poor in order that they might be sustained. If you do not understand that God desires to bless you with financial wealth, then you are missing out on one of the great promises of the Bible. When you plant seeds into the life of others, you experience the fullness of the rewards and blessings that have been reserved with your name on them.

How willing am I to give to those in need?

____

____

____

____

____

Personal Notes/Reflection

Life Application:

1. Generosity comes from the heart.
2. You are called to serve others with generosity.

Chapter 19: Dare to Dream Big

Joel 2:28-29 (CSB) - After this, I will pour out My Spirit on all humanity; then your sons and your daughters will prophesy, your old men will have dreams, and your young men will see visions. I will even pour out My Spirit on the male and female slaves in those days.

God wants you to dream and to dream big!

While God was forming you, and before He placed you in the womb, He made deposits of His dream for your life into your heart. The dream is His plan for your destiny. These dreams are the purpose for which you were born. God poured visions and dreams into your heart so you could live a life filled with purpose.

Dreams are a picture of the life you can have. They are fantasies of what you can become. Many of you have sat for hours watching movies you enjoy. These movies bring to life what is in someone's imagination. They take the vision from their imagination and bring it to life with crystal clarity.

God has given you a great imagination so you can create pictures or movies of the great life He has planned for you. Your imagination helps you to dream about the future and what you hope to accomplish. The visions you see in your imagination are the outpouring of God's Spirit, which will catapult you into your divine destiny.

You must begin to envision the great life and destiny God has mapped out for you so that you can begin the necessary preparation to attain it.

How have I been productively or unproductively the use of my imagination?

____

____

____

____

____

Discovering your Dream

Jeremiah 1: 5 – Before I formed thee in the belly I knew thee; and before thou camest forth out of the womb I sanctified thee, and I ordained thee a prophet unto the nations.

All of you have been given a dream by God. If you are alive, then you have been given a dream to fulfill.

I have often heard it said that the richest place on earth is the graveyard because many people died without accomplishing the dreams that God placed in their hearts. God not only gave you dreams, but He has planned a time frame for their fulfillment.

If you are thinking right now, I don't have a dream, think again. God did not forget a single one of you as He planted and distributed dreams. You were handpicked and selected to fulfill something in His Kingdom, whether small or great. Something has been stirring in your soul that will not let go of you. Try as you may to bury it, it keeps rising to the surface. This desire to do something is the desire to complete the dream assignment that God so carefully planted in your heart.

Many of you have tried to suppress this desire, and you often think you were successful, just to realize later it was only buried for a season. There are others who have used excuses because you believe you are not talented or gifted enough to succeed. You have a hard time believing the things God is speaking to your heart. God is not looking at your talents or gifts because He plans to do the accomplishing in you.

If you will surrender to Him and to the dream, He reveals to you, the dream will indeed come to pass without delay.

What dream has God deposited in your heart?

____

____

____

____

____

The Price to Dream Big

Ecclesiastes 3:1 – There is an occasion for everything, and a time for every activity under heaven.

There is a price tag for dreaming big!

As you begin to dream, you are often unaware that you will pay a price to accomplish your dreams. I have discovered that many people spend countless hours in the preparation process. Some sacrifice and work tirelessly to accomplish their dreams; still others have to lay down their life for what they believe.

There is always a sacrifice for dreaming big and accomplishing those dreams. The price may look steep as you begin, but the rewards are worth the sacrifice.

The key to success in the dreaming process is to plant seeds into another person's dream while yours is developing. Sow your time into others and help them to overcome the struggles they face while working on their dreams. When you plant seeds into another person's dream and vision, you will reap a harvest in your life when you need it the most.

As you begin walking toward your dream, there will be a time of planting, seedtime, and harvest. God plants the idea into your heart, you allow the idea to take root and germinate, and then you begin to seed into the idea by planning and preparing to accomplish it. After the planting there will eventually come a harvest if you do not neglect the seed.

You must continue to water it, even during the dry seasons when it appears lifeless. Beneath the surface of your dreams, growth and life are taking place even though you cannot see them with the naked eye.

How much are you willing to sacrifice to attain your dream?

____

____

____

Personal Notes/Reflection

Life Application:

1. Generosity comes from the heart.
2. You are called to serve others with generosity.

Chapter 20: Obstacles to Your Dreams

1 Corinthians 15:58 – Therefore my beloved brethren, be ye steadfast, unmovable, always abounding in the work of the Lord, forasmuch as ye know that your labor is not in vain in the Lord.

You will face some challenges and obstacles from time to time on your way to the fulfillment of your dream. When you face these challenges, you must make the decision to persevere.

Perseverance will be the key that unlocks the door and gives you entry. As you approach your dreams, you may be challenged by lack. Often you may lack the resources you need to begin the process. You may also find that you do not have the necessary help in the beginning phase. Some of you will discover that you may not have the necessary skills or knowledge about where to start. Others' dreams may seem hopeless at first, especially when there are adverse circumstances surrounding them.

You will face some time alone and some loneliness in the process of preparing the groundwork for your dreams. Sometimes when you get to your dreams, it may appear that they are occupied, as was the case with the children of Israel. When they arrived at their Promised Land, giants, unholy, and ungodly people were occupying it; and they knew that it would require a sacrifice and a fight to take occupancy. They had to prepare for outright war in order to take the land.

Many of them were fainthearted not remembering that God was on their side and that He would bring ultimate victory. God is on your side and will bring you ultimate victory, so do not let fear hinder your progress.

What obstacles have been hindering me?

____

____

____

____

____

Distractions

Ephesians 2:10 – For we are his workmanship, created in Christ Jesus unto good works, which God hath before ordained that we should walk in them.

It is amazing to me that the very moment you decide to get serious about your destiny is the moment when difficulties begin to manifest in your life. You will run into obstacles and situations with your family and friends that call for your immediate attention.

The enemy uses distractions to keep you disorientated and unfocused. Distractions break your focus and keep you off center. You are then unable to settle in and begin working on the things that are necessary to bring about your destiny.

Distractions are a ploy of the enemy to keep you unproductive and in the same cycle day in and day out. You must learn to recognize his attacks and be prepared to counterattack when necessary.

The key to not being caught off guard is to be prayed up and prepared so, as he attempts to distract and dissuade you, you are one step ahead of his ploy.

Learn to stay focused when distractions come your way by keeping your eyes fixed on Jesus and continuing to follow the instructions He has given to you. If you focus on Him, you will be able to see the solutions you are looking for quickly and clearly.

What is distracting you from your goal?

____

____

____

____

____

Delays

Galatians 6: 9 - And let us not be weary in well doing for in due season we shall reap, if we faint not.

The weapon of delay can bring discouragement to all of us. It appears as if you are always waiting on something. Often you are waiting on God's timing or waiting on help from family and friends or even for the right doors to open for you.

In this waiting process, you often feel as if these delays will hamper your progress; but delays are not always denials, and you must learn to stand firm in the waiting season. When you encounter delays, you tend to be less motivated about exploring other options because you are wondering whether it is worth it.

Delays keep you believing it was not meant to be, and that nothing good ever happens to you, so why spend the energy trying? The ploy of delay is to keep you living a mediocre existence and to be content with only a limited supply. Delay will keep you from believing that all things are possible with God.

You must shake off this weight by pressing into God more and more. Spend time thanking Him for your blessings, which are on the way. Praise Him when you do not yet see the answers! If He has not said "No," then rest assured the answer is definitely on the way. You will get the breakthrough you need as you learn that perseverance is necessary to get from God what He has in store for you.

In what areas are you experiencing delays?

____

____

____

____

____

Disappointment

Proverb 15:22 – Without counsel purpose are disappointed; but in the multitude of counselors they are established.

Disappointments come to us in many forms. You might be disappointed because your life is not the way you planned it. Nothing seems to go your way. You keep trying and trying without success, and you just want to yell at the top of your lungs, "Let me off this spinning wheel, this is not what I signed up for."

When you are disappointed, you feel sorry for yourself and have some of the greatest pity parties. Poor me, no one cares, nothing I do works! In the midst of your "poor me" syndrome, you cannot feel the encouragement of the Holy Spirit telling you to shake it off and encouraging you to look for the good in all situations. Disappointments cloud your view, and you cannot get a clear picture of where you are or where you are going.

The key to letting go of disappointments is to believe that your steps are ordered of the Lord and that He is leading you to the fulfillment of your dreams.

I traveled a lot in a previous job, and many times prior to take off it would be stormy and cloudy on the ground. The moment we rose above the clouds, to our surprise, many times the sun would be shining. God has used this illustration in my life to remind me that the situation is never hopeless, but that I must get a Kingdom perspective on it. My perspective was too limited; therefore, I was limited by it.

What keeps me living with disappointments?

____

____

____

____

____

Discouragement

Psalm 42:5 – Why are thou cast down, O my soul? And why art thou disquieted in me? Hope thou in God, for I shall yet praise Him for the help of His countenance.

Discouragement comes when you have failed in your attempt to accomplish something. The enemy tells you that you are the only one who keeps failing and never passing the test. You have to keep in mind that he is a liar and the father of lies. Therefore, do not believe him when he tells you that you are the only one who has missed it. He wants you down and out for the count.

When you accept discouragement, you become very lethargic, unconcerned, and unmoved about what is taking place around you. Your courage fails you in the midst of your crisis. Nothing seems to move you, and you are not willing to give it another try. You give up more easily on your dreams when you are discouraged because you believe you cannot accomplish them. It seems that every time you try nothing happens.

You must resist the spirit of discouragement and remind yourself that you are the head and not the tail and that you will not allow it to ruin the plans God has for you. The Bible tells us that the Kingdom of Heaven suffers violence and the violent take it by force (Matt.11:12). What you need to do is to become violent about the destruction and pain the enemy brings to your life. You must let him know in no uncertain terms that enough is enough, and you will not allow him to have rule or control in any area of your life.

What is causing me to be discouraged?

____

____

____

____

____

Despair

Revelation 12:11 – And they overcame him by the blood of the Lamb, and the word of their testimony; and they loved not their lives unto the death.

Despair is a reality for many people. You suffer despair when you have endured great losses. Despair comes in many forms; and, when you encounter it, you are often unaware of what is going on around you so you merely exist in a fog. Often you are so lost in despair that you are unconcerned about life and what it still has to offer you.

Despair brings a feeling of hopelessness, which can feel unbreakable at times. The enemy's ploy is to keep you so devastated that you cannot run the race that has been set before you. Despair does not have to be a stronghold in your life because you have the power of God on your side to overcome it and to keep it from taking up residence in your life.

Each day you must make a decision to fight the spirit of despair and to pull it down. Remember to take every thought captive and bring it under the authority of the Lord Jesus Christ. Take captive the thoughts of despair by submitting them to God who will bring healing and wholeness back to your life.

All of these obstacles have been sent to derail you and to keep you from fulfilling your destiny. These things are dream-killers, and if you allow them to take root in your heart, they will choke the life out of your dream. The Bible declares that the Greater One lives in you. You have the power to overcome because of the Blood of the Lamb and the word of your testimony (Rev. 12:11). The blood of Jesus purchased your victory at Calvary.

Personal Notes/Reflection

Life Application:

1. Generosity comes from the heart.
2. You are called to serve others with generosity.

Chapter 21: A Life–Changing Decision

Isaiah 58:7 (CSB) - Is it not to share your bread with the hungry, to bring the poor and homeless into your house, to clothe the naked when you see him, and to not ignore your own flesh and blood?

You have all been given the opportunity to make a life-changing decision at one time or another. This decision has altered the course of your destiny.

When God called you to dream big and filled your heart with visions of what you could become, you had the opportunity at that moment to make a life-changing decision. For every dream God has given you, realize that the dream was given to fulfill a purpose in Him. You have been given dreams to meet the needs of others, to bring hope to the hopeless, and to feed the hungry. Your dream will provide shelter for the homeless and clothing to the naked.

God has called you to dream big so you can be His hands and feet to a world that is in need of Him. As you begin to embrace your dreams and look for the possibilities in them, you must have a willingness to put your all on the line to accomplish them. You will not always know what the outcome might be, but you must trust that God will be with you every step of the way.

Faith, courage, and hope are key ingredients to your dream-fulfillment. There will be giants along the way that will challenge your faith, hope, and courage, but you have power to look them in the eye and still make the decision that you can do all things through Christ who strengthens you.

Do not allow limitations in your dreams and your thinking, but be willing to bend and sway with the changes that may come. Sometimes changes come to allow you to see a different set of opportunities. You will discover that if you are willing to dream and can believe God in the process, then nothing will be impossible to you.

What life-changing decision must you make for your destiny?

____

____

____

____

____

Rahab

Joshua 2:1-6 (CSB) - Joshua, son of Nun, secretly sent two men as spies from Acacia Grove, saying, "Go and scout the land, especially Jericho." So they left, and they came to the house of a woman, a prostitute named Rahab, and stayed there. The King of Jericho was told, "Look, some of the Israelite men have come here tonight to investigate the land." Then the King of Jericho sent word to Rahab and said, "Bring out the men who came to you and entered your house, for they came to investigate the entire land." But the woman had taken the two men and hidden them. So she said, "Yes, the men did come to me, but I didn't know where they were from. At nightfall, when the gate was about to close, the men went out, and I don't know where they were going. Chase after them quickly, and you can catch up with them!" But she had taken them up to the roof and hidden them among the stalks of flax that she had arranged on the roof.

Rahab, a prostitute, made a decision that was to change the course of her life and her destiny. I have come to the conclusion that she was one of the wisest women in the Bible. She saw an opportunity and grabbed hold of it with both hands.

As seen in the above passage, she hid the two spies and kept them from being captured and killed. Once the danger passed, she helped them to escape from one of the windows in her house, using a scarlet rope.

Here is why I think she was smart. Before she released them, she extracted a promise from them that when they came in to take over the city, they would save her and her family. They promised her that if all of her family members were in the house with her when they came through and the scarlet cord was hanging from the same window through, which she had let them down, her household would be saved. Here entire family was saved because she followed the spies' instructions.

What are you willing to do for God?

____

____

____

____

____

Rahab's Blessings

Hebrews 11:31 – By faith the harlot Rahab perished not with them that believed not, when she received the spies with peace.

Now get a hold of this picture. The prostitute Rahab and her family were taken into the Israeli camp to live among the people. Can you imagine how the prostitute was dressed and what she looked like among those holy virgin women?

God in His infinite grace, mercy, and love had compassion on this prostitute who was willing to be used by Him. Even though she had lived in prostitution, when she encountered God, she allowed God to use the brokenness of her life to bring deliverance to His people.

God took her into the Israeli camp, and Salmon, one of the spies who were sent into Jericho, bypassed all the other women in his tribe and married Rahab. One of Joshua's top leaders married the prostitute because it was in God's divine plan.

If that was all God did for Rahab that alone would have been a blessing in her life. God, however, did not stop there in His destiny for her. Rahab and Salmon had children and in Matthew 1, we find Rahab in the genealogy of Jesus Christ. God did not conclude Rahab's story there.

In Hebrews 11, you see that Rahab was the only other woman besides Sarah, Abraham's wife, who was listed in the famous hall of faith. God took a prostitute who probably had no dream or vision for her life and used the broken pieces not only to deliver His people but to deliver her as well. He forgave, cleansed, and put her on a new path to a destiny she never imagined or dared to dream. He did not waste a single thing that happened in her life. He took all of the brokenness, used it for His glory, and then gave her a testimony, which has been told for centuries, just because she was willing to yield to Him. He worked all things together for her good and transformed her life.

How will you experience the abundant blessings of God?

____

____

____

____

____

Rahab's Example

Hebrews 11:6 – but without faith it is impossible to please him; for he that cometh to God must believe that he is and that he is a rewarded of them that diligently seek him.

Rahab walked in faith and her life was transformed as a result of her walk. God gave her an abundance of blessings, provision, love and forgiveness. He used her because she was willing to let go of the things in her life that were producing no results.

As you ponder on the awesomeness of God, consider that if God could use a prostitute to fulfill such greatness to bring glory to Himself, and He is no respecter of persons, then He will do the same for you.

All you are required to do is to make a life-changing decision and say, "Yes" to Him. He will also take the broken pieces of your life, give you a new dream and vision, and then use you to fulfill the greatest destiny He planned for your life.

He will use you without fail if you will dare to dream big. Like Abraham, Joseph, Rahab, and many other well-known men and women of our time, if you will embrace God's promises, stand on His Word, and never give up, you will accomplish all that you were called, chosen, and destined to do.

What example are you leaving for others to follow?

____

____

____

____

____

Personal Notes/Reflection

Life Application:

1. Generosity comes from the heart.
2. You are called to serve others with generosity.

A Proclamation

I am a child of the King. I will begin to embrace the great plans and destiny He has for my life. I will let nothing stop me from attaining all that He birthed me to accomplish. I will stop living below His promises for my life. From this day forward, I am on a new course to my destiny. I will not be stopped or deterred, and I will live my life to the fullest by honoring God in everything that I do. I will begin my treasure hunt to find out what God has deposited in my life. When I discover His plan for me, I will begin to move toward those plans. I will glorify God in all that I do and bring honor to His Kingdom. Amen!

A Confession

Father, I know that without you I am lost and without hope. I ask Jesus to come into my life and make His home in me. I repent of my sins and turn back to you. Please forgive me and wash me clean. I open my heart to you and ask you to come and live your life in and through me. From this day forward, I will live entirely for you. I will not look back on my past but fully accept your forgiveness and embrace my future. Thank You that Jesus is now the Savior of my life. Amen!

Notes

1. Chapter 4, 12, 17

Rick Renner, Sparkling Gems from the Greek
(Tulsa, OK: Teach all Nations, 2003)

2. Chapter 19
The Dream Giver, Bruce Wilkinson
Multnomah Publishers Sisters, Oregon

Other Books by Joan E. Murray

Flow Through Me, Lord

Called and Chosen for Destiny

Workbook: Called and Chosen for Destiny

Show Me How to Love

Faith that Conquers

Hope in Difficult Seasons

I Must Pray

Lord, Make Me Whole

Lord, Make Me Whole (Spanish)

Overcoming Loneliness and Aloneness

Reconnect

Boldness in Christ

Time In Life's Waiting Room

Winning In the Battles of Life

Workbook: Winning in the Battles of Life

Worship Our Deepest Need

You Can Trust Him

Workbook: You Can Trust Him

Other Resources

https://joanmurrayministries.org/
https://jemmuniquegifts.com
https://linktr.ee/joanmurrayministries

My gift to you
PRAYERS That Produce Results

https://joanmurrayministries.org/prayers/praying-the-word-of-god/

If you would like to know more about Joan Murray Ministries, please contact us at:

Joan Murray Ministries
P.O. Box 5073
Katy, TX 77491
281-398-2501

email: jmmcontactus@gmail.com
www.JoanMurrayMinistries.org
www.jemmuniquegifts.com

Changing Lives Through the Power and Truth of God's Word.

About The Author

Joan Murray is totally committed to helping people discover their destinies. She is the founder and CEO of Joan Murray Ministries and Seeds of Hope Worldwide Missions. Joan is dedicated to teaching, training, equipping and helping people who are in various life struggles.

Joan is an international Bible teacher, pastor, author, and missionary. She has travelled extensively throughout the United States and internationally sharing the gospel message and serving the needs of the downtrodden. Joan currently resides in Houston, Texas.

www.ingramcontent.com/pod-product-compliance
Lightning Source LLC
Chambersburg PA
CBHW080345030726
47598CB00009B/2641

* 9 7 8 1 9 6 3 0 1 6 2 5 3 *